THE
Winning Family

*Increasing Self-Esteem
in Your Children and Yourself*

Dr. Louise Hart

Illustrated by *Kristen Baumgardner*

CELESTIALARTS

This book is dedicated to my children, Damian, Kristen, and Felix Baumgardner, with gratitude and love. Over the years, they have been my best teachers and cheerleaders. It is also dedicated to the many parents who have shared their struggles, successes, and insights.

My special thanks to my daughter, Kristen Baumgardner, for her superb editing and wonderful cartoon illustrations. I appreciate her dependability and skill in helping me put onto paper the concepts that are closest to my heart.

♣

Celestial Arts
P.O. Box 7123
Berkeley, California 94707

Text design by Lynn Meinhardt
Cover design by Ken Scott
Type set by Archetype, Berkeley

Library of Congress Cataloging-in-Publication Data

Hart, Louise.
    The winning family : increasing self-esteem in your children and
    yourself / Louise Hart. — Rev.
        p. cm.
    Includes bibliographical references and index.
    ISBN 0-89087-689-4
    1. Self-esteem.   2. Self-esteem in children.   3. Child rearing.
    I. Title.
    BF697.5.S46H37   1993
    649'.7—dc20   93-6844
                                                       CIP

Printed in the United States of America
FIRST CELESTIAL ARTS PRINTING 1993

        4   5   6   7   8   9   10   —   97   96

Contents

Preface

I wish this book had been available to me twenty years ago—and to my mother forty years ago, and to her mother before that. But we cannot turn back time. We must begin where we are now and move forward.

The biological parent-child connection is the deepest natural bond there is. It continues even after separation by death. From the moment they first appear, children introduce a new dimension to our lives that expands, challenges, deepens, sweetens, and at times exhausts us. Our children present us with ongoing opportunities to grow.

I write as a parent who has been there—stretching and growing in the process of my own life—and also as a community psychologist trying to prevent mental illness by teaching life skills for building healthier, happier individuals and families.

Like many people today, I have lived in a variety of family structures. When I was born, my mother ran the household while my father worked outside the home. I had the benefit of living in an extended family and had relatives other than my parents as models. After college I got married and taught school for four years.

With my pregnancy, I entered the full-time-profession of a stay-at-home mom, a common role in times past. That situation gave me the opportunity to lay the groundwork for this book. I had more time to sort through some of the challenges of raising kids than today's parents have. As I mothered my daughter and two sons, I discovered and confronted issues from my own childhood, and learned to heal my own "inner child" in the process.

My young family settled in Colorado. My mother, brothers, and sister lived a thousand miles to the east and the west, so there was very little contact with grandparents, aunts, uncles, and cousins. We functioned as the typical nuclear family in isolation from extended family for several years, until my husband's parents moved out west to be near their grandchildren.

Now my family has yet another form. After living for several years in a single-parent household, my three children are now attending college, working, and discovering the world, while my presentations on self-esteem and parenting take me across the country and beyond. Living separately, we look forward to our reunions with joy and excitement. My daughter and I have also had the opportunity to stretch our roles even further in a business relationship.

Families come in many diverse forms and sizes, from large, extended families to the "family of one." Over the course of a lifetime, a person might live in all of these. Regardless of living arrangements, deep connections will always link family members.

This book can be helpful for any person, from any type of family, who is ready to let go of dysfunctional patterns and reach for health, joy, and satisfaction; who believes that everyone can be a winner in his or her own right and that no one has to lose out. The information is relevant to anyone who is part of a family. It speaks to parents of all populations, to child-care providers, and to educators. It is helpful to anyone who works with or cares for children—or has been a child.

A winning family begins with good intentions. Yet good intentions are not enough. We must reexamine what we know about raising children. We need to learn from old mistakes rather than repeat them. We need to be willing to examine and replace negative habits and patterns in our lives. Raising our children differently can help us heal the wounds of the past.

A tennis pro once said, "If your game's not working, change it." This book is for those who are ready to take the step toward conscious parenting. Being part of a family should be a loving and enjoyable experience.

With three children of my own, I have come to learn that parents have a great deal of influence over children's lives; we hold the reins for family rules, communication styles, and the emotional climate in the family. Of course, there are areas in which we have little or no control. All children are born with their own personalities and special purpose in the world. Some are born with gifts or talents that require extra attention. Others have physical or mental challenges that require an atmosphere of support and empowerment to keep them from being victims of their differences.

The cultural climate also profoundly affects us. We are defined by it, yet at the same time we also create it. Seen in this light, society can limit or expand us, entrap or enhance us. If we can clearly identify dangers and opportunities, we can give our children the power to cope with problems and challenges, to make conscious choices instead of being victims.

The Winning Family delves into commonly encountered problems and offers healthy solutions. It teaches important skills to effectively meet the challenges of living with and raising kids in a complex world. This book can help you build your house on a firm foundation.

It has always been difficult to raise healthy kids, but the challenge is greater today than in the 1960s when my children were small. Rarely do parents have the automatic support that was built into extended families in times past. Seldom do they get encouragement for the nurturing qualities that are essential for good parenting. Yet the way we raise our children affects the world in the present and in the future.

There is no one right way to parent; there are many. You need to find the way that works best for you. Become an expert on your family—you know them better than anyone else. Trust

yourself. Take good care of yourself, for your own sake and for the sake of the people with whom you share your life.

Nor is there one right way to use this book. Some people read it all the way through in one sitting. Others take it bit by bit over a long period of time, applying the techniques to their families day by day. The greatest rewards come from putting what is learned into practice.

These skills work not only in raising a family of your own, but also in healing your family of origin. Here is a moving example: A father, estranged from his five children for some fifteen years, visited his son with the hope of bringing the family together again. They all gathered, tentatively, using this book as a springboard to begin to talk through some of the old wounds and to shed light on their relationships. The grudges, suspicions, and resentment that had pushed them apart for so many years are now dispersing. With new tools to understand each other and themselves, a great healing is taking place. These strangers are reweaving the broken web and taking the first, most difficult steps towards re-creating their family.

However you choose to use this book, I support you and believe in you. And I thank you for working to shape a better world for our children, our grandchildren, and all future generations.

Louise Hart ♡

Fifty years from now,
it will not matter
what kind of car you drove,
what kind of house you lived in,
how much you had in your bank account,
or what your clothes looked like.
But the world will be
a little better because
you were important
in the life of a child.

Anonymous

1

You Are Building a Cathedral

"Our children give us the opportunity to become the parents we always wished we'd had."

Louise Hart

Many years ago, two men were working at the same job on the outskirts of a European city. A stranger approached them and asked, "What are you doing?" The first man replied with an edge of resentment, "I'm hauling rocks." The second man enthusiastically replied, "I'm building a cathedral!"

Just as skilled craftsmen designed cathedrals to be inspiring, to stand tall and strong, and to resist the elements over the years, we who raise and teach and care for children are working to build in them the strength and skills to live happy, creative, productive lives. This vitally important work is too often unsupported and undervalued.

Raising healthy children is the most important work of the culture. If you have children, parenting is your most important job. What you do when your children are small will contribute to the pain or the joy of the rest of your life. Little other work has such far-reaching effects, influencing present and future generations alike.

We are the products of our families, our culture, and our time—and of these three, family has the strongest influence. My parents gave me more than they ever received. As children, they had had difficult times in Germany. The first of twelve children, my mother grew up with adult responsibilities. Her mother had died delivering the fourth baby, and her father's new wife continued to have and raise children.

The primary focus in that family was survival; the primary value was work. My parents transmitted those values to us. With the best of intentions, they did all they could for their children, but they couldn't give what they didn't have. My mother once asked, "How can I love when I never was loved?" She talked about how much she had always missed the love of her own mother. History, unfortunately, tends to repeat itself.

Many people operate under the assumption that since parenting is a natural adult function, we should instinctively know how to do it—and do it well. The truth is, effective parenting requires study and practice like any other skilled profession. Who would even consider turning an untrained surgeon loose in an operating room? Yet we "operate" on our children every day.

Things just weren't right for me as a child. I was confused, lost, and lonely. I felt unloved. I had no self-esteem—I had no sense of self. When I was pregnant with my first child in the early 1960s, I made the most important decision of my life: a commitment to raise my children the way I would like to have been raised. This was not easy to do since I had no models. I became (as did other parents around me) a pioneer. After examining and reexamining everything I knew about parenting, I gave my kids what I thought was best.

My children, now young adults, are basically healthy, happy, responsible individuals with good self-esteem. What continues to delight me is that I receive from them what I have given: acceptance, respect, love, and support. Children deserve the best, and *over time, what goes around comes around.*

As children, we had no choice about how we were parented. As parents, we have the choice to repeat the patterns used with us *unconsciously,* or to *consciously* pass on only those values we would like to see perpetuated.

For better or worse, you probably learned how to parent from your parents. You were taught by the examples they set; they were what you learned. If you felt loved and valued as a child and if you've become a competent, healthy adult, you were fortunate to have had good modeling. Thank your parents. Raising kids should be relatively easy for you. But if you do not like the way you were raised—if you were rejected, neglected, or abused in any way, if you grew up in an alcoholic or other dysfunctional family system—you can choose differently. *You can rise above old, destructive patterns* to create a healthy life for yourself and your family.

A good place to start is by taking an honest look at your own childhood. Remember what it was like growing up in your family. What did your parents do to make you feel loved? How did they discipline you? How did they communicate and resolve problems with you and with each other? What helped you to feel good about yourself, and what led you to conclude that you were "bad," that there was something wrong with you? Try not to idealize your experiences. Glossing over painful memories leaves you at greater risk of repeating those behaviors with your own children.

We learned to parent from our mothers and fathers. Being human, they made mistakes. *We can choose to learn from those mistakes rather than passing them on. We can choose to heal ourselves rather than wounding our children.*

To become conscious parents, we need to question, sift, and sort through old "tapes," habits, and patterns. *Pass on the best—and throw away the rest.* This commitment is our best assurance that whatever negative patterns we may have grown up with will not be repeated in our children's generation.

We live in an exciting time. More and more parents are becoming conscious of how they are parenting. Today we are becoming more and more aware of the impact our choices have on our children's future. *With awareness comes choice.* We can choose to look back at our childhoods, identify the consequences of various parenting strategies, and sort them into "growthful" or "harmful." Then we can pick the ones we want to hand down to our own children.

Both negative and positive experiences contribute to our parenting skills. It's like the "Twenty Questions" game: A no is every bit as valuable as a yes because it helps us narrow the field of options. If we insist on denying any pain or suffering we may have experienced, we run the risk of unconsciously repeating painful behaviors with our children—even if we swore we never would. We have all felt wounded at times. Instead of wounding our own children, let's use our love for them as an inspiration to heal ourselves.

Give your children what you want back. If you respect and accept them, they will learn to respect and accept; if you abuse and reject them, they will learn to abuse and reject. It's like a hug: You have to give one away if you want to get one back. Be there for your kids when they're young and they'll probably be there for you when you're old.

Children are natural imitators. They reflect how you think, how you love, what you value, how you solve problems, what you do with feelings, and how you deal with others in the world. Whether you know it or not, you are teaching self-esteem—or a lack of it—to your children all the time. So be your best self, and they will want to become their best, too. Self-esteem in families begins with who you are.

Since we can't give what we don't have, we need to learn how to raise our own self-esteem along with our children's. Self-esteem is the greatest gift a parent can give to a child. Parents can lay a solid, loving foundation early in the lives of their children that builds inner strength and resiliency before the outside world has a major impact. The old saying, "an ounce of prevention is worth a pound of cure," certainly applies to self-esteem.

Parents can help *prevent low self-esteem*—and keep their loved ones from

- educational failure
- vulnerability to negative peer pressure
- drug and alcohol abuse
- teen pregnancy
- dropping out of school
- eating disorders
- other addictive behaviors
- battering relationships
- crime and violence
- suicide

and parents can *promote high self-esteem* so that their children

- resist dependencies and addictions
- are enthusiastic about life (and school!)
- make friends easily
- trust themselves
- are self-directed
- are cooperative and follow reasonable rules
- take pride in their achievements
- are basically happy individuals
- are an asset to society and to the world!

Parenting gives you an opportunity to create joy and love. It also encourages you to develop desirable personal qualities (such as patience), to understand and appreciate *yourself* at deeper levels, and to learn new skills. Your children become your best teachers.

One mother, Anne, said, "My lessons began with bonding. As I held my beautiful baby, I experienced a totally unconditional love between us, and a wonderful sense of euphoria. I was aware and appreciative of my uniqueness. My twenty-two-month-old son has taught me so many lessons. He's taught me what love is, he's taught me self-acceptance, and he's taught me to relax and let him go through his stages."

As parents we need to provide a loving, safe home for our children. We also need to face the fact that our larger Home—the planet—is in crisis. Healing the planet is essential if we care about the future for our children and our children's children. This is an enormous responsibility and an exciting challenge. Working with others, we can help fashion a new, healthy world. We can raise our children to become healthy adults who will join us in creating a more positive and peaceful world for everyone.

2

The Greatest Gift: Self-Esteem

"What a man thinks of himself, that it is
which determines, or rather indicates his fate."[1]

Henry David Thoreau

We make healthy children by working from the inside out—by cherishing and accepting them as they are and nurturing their growth and development. "We make butterflies by feeding caterpillars, not by trying to paste wings on them."[2]

Self-esteem means holding yourself in esteem and knowing you are worthwhile. In affirming your dignity, you know that you have the right to be treated with respect. You have the right to be happy. Self-esteem involves a sense of personal

competence and confidence in one's ability to deal with life. Self-esteem leads to harmony.

People commonly try to gain a sense of importance by being one-up over others. This stems from egotism. When you are okay with yourself, you don't need to make others wrong. People who feel good about themselves don't have to put others down. Egotism thrives on conflict.

Many people think that self-esteem comes from others or from something external. They may believe that someone else is responsible for their happiness. The fact is that for adults *self*-esteem is something you give to your*self.*

Only *you* can give yourself *self*-respect.
Only *you* can give yourself *self*-acceptance.
Only *you* can give yourself *self*-esteem.

Typically, however, people with low self-esteem try to prove they're okay through external sources, by

- **What they do.** Many people get their self-esteem through work or through doing things for others. They shift from being human beings to human doings. They may be workaholics.
- **What they have.** "He who dies with the most toys wins," reads a bumper sticker. Some people crave material possessions and can never get enough. Competing with the Joneses, their "stuff" and debts control their lives.
- **What they know.** Many people try to impress others with information and with the many books they have read.
- **How they perform.** Many people are acutely aware of how they affect others. They operate their lives attempting to achieve a desired effect on others.
- **How they look.** Many people put a great amount of time, effort, and money into their appearance.

- **Who they are with.** Many people think they have to have a "good" partner in order to be okay.

The ultimate hope is that others will notice and approve of them; *then* they will be okay. Their self-esteem is based on external conditions. They are people pleasers and approval seekers who have given others the power to control their self-esteem. This "self"-esteem is conditional. For example, "If I do ____, I am okay." "If I look beautiful, I am okay." "If I act ____, I am okay." Conversely, "If I don't do ____, I am not okay." Not that these acts or qualities don't have value. We need to do things and to look after our appearance. We need to be smart and to have possessions. We need to choose our friends and associates carefully. The problem arises when we *need to* impress or please others—when we depend on the approval of others in order to feel okay.

Such external sources of self-esteem are not solid. We don't know when to stop. I may feel okay today because I have a bigger boat than the Joneses; yet tomorrow they might buy an even better one. I may feel okay today because I've read every book on the best-seller list; yet next month I may not have time. Or I may feel okay because I did a thousand things for my family; yet if I stop doing all those things (possibly because of exhaustion), then I'm not okay and my self-esteem drops.

Self-esteem is not what you do or know; it is not based on your appearance or how much money you have. *Self-esteem is based on who you are.* As you accept, respect, and cherish yourself more, you can take charge of your own self-esteem and stop working so hard to prove it by pleasing others. By becoming more pleasing to yourself, you regard yourself more highly, and become more endearing to others in the process.

Unconditional self-esteem is based on unconditional love for yourself. The First Commandment tells us to love our neighbors as ourselves. This means that we should first love ourselves, then love our neighbors (and our children). In reality, if I hate myself, I can't love my kids, my friends, or my neighbors. If I believe that I am not lovable, it's hard to imagine that my kids or anyone else might really love me—even when they do.

Self-esteem begins with a choice, plus a change of "self-talk" and a change of heart. Positive self-esteem comes from making the commitment to respect, accept, and love yourself completely. It is the best gift you can give to yourself—and your children. This gift is in your hands.

Self-esteem evolves through the quality of the relationships between children and those who are important in their lives. For the most part, children look to the adults in their environment (and later to their peers) for a reflection of who and how they are. Keen observers, they soak up every bit of information we provide—our words, facial expressions, posture, tone of voice, touch. They notice how we react and respond to them: whether their physical and emotional needs are met, whether they are taken seriously and listened to, whether they are respected and enjoyed. They observe, then draw conclusions. ("I am important," "I don't matter," "I am loved," "I'm a nuisance.")

Their conclusions become their truth, their basic beliefs about who they are and what they deserve in life. Sometimes their conclusions are faulty. For example, children may conclude that they are responsible for their parents' divorce. Yet their "truth" is not true. A parent leaves a marriage because of difficulties with a spouse, not with a child.

Children tend to view parents and authority figures as all knowing and all powerful. They think, "Those important people treat me as I deserve to be treated. What they say about me is what I am." When children are respected, they conclude that they *deserve* respect; they develop self-respect. When they are treated with esteem, when they are cherished, they conclude that they *deserve* esteem, and they develop self-esteem. On the other hand, if they are neglected or abused, they conclude that they deserve *that*—that they have it coming; they conclude that they are bad because they would not be treated badly if they were good. It then becomes easy for them to allow others to mistreat them. Parents are, in effect, like mirrors. What we reflect back to our children becomes the basis for their self-image. It influences every aspect of their lives.

The truth is, no one deserves abuse or harmful punishment. No one deserves to be hit. No one deserves to be abandoned. Every single child—every single person—deserves and needs respect, acceptance, and unconditional love. A parent's job is to fill these needs.

This is particularly the case when children have special needs that make them "different." When the world sees a child who is physically or mentally handicapped or gifted, or as an ethnic minority or lower status, the child is indirectly harmed. Although terms like "handicapped" continue to be used to describe physical or mental challenges, for example, the attitudes behind the words are the danger. Our words can carry deep connotations that may have more impact than is intended. Children identify with the labels you give them, and may develop a poor self-image and low self-esteem if they are given the wrong ones.

If we view our children as being somehow "broken" or as having a "deficit," this image works against them. If we can honestly see them, instead, as having both strengths and challenges, it allows them simply to be unique. Which they are. *Everyone has differences; some are just more apparent than others.* All children have certain areas in which they need extra support and encouragement in order to succeed and foster a positive self-image and self-esteem.[3]

Fostering self-esteem in a child from the outset is easier and healthier than trying to repair damaged self-esteem later in life. Yet we cannot turn back the clock. We must start where we are now. If your children are older, it's not too late. *The same things that build self-esteem in the first place also repair damaged self-esteem later on*—for your children and yourself. Now is the time to increase self-esteem. A new approach, new skills, and a dash of compassion can begin the healing process.

A thirty-five-year-old woman told me that she barely spoke to her mother from the time she was about eight or nine until she was twenty-six and divorcing her first husband. Only then did they begin to share feelings, to develop a sense of trust in each other, to work through some of the misunderstandings and unintentional hurts that had come between them. Today they have a warm, supportive, and loving relationship.

It is easier to develop self-esteem if you know how to go about it. Good intentions start you on the right path. But you need information and new skills to do things differently. As little as five minutes a day trying out new strategies with your children can produce positive changes.

So what do you do first? Self-esteem begins with self-love, with respecting, accepting, and taking care of *yourself.* That love spills over to your children, who learn to love themselves and to love you. *Love cures people—those who give it and those who receive it.*

Where does self-esteem begin with children? With bonding. A most critical and wonderful event occurs naturally when a newborn infant and parents have skin-to-skin and other sensory contact. With nursing, cooing, touching, rocking, and cuddling, a newborn bonds quickly to mother and father. This primal attachment is the foundation for trust, for love, for self-esteem and healthy development. Through bonding with our children, we can heal

incomplete bonding with our mothers and fathers. We can reconnect with our inner child and begin a process of deep personal healing.

If you had difficulty with early bonding, or if you adopted, there are always other opportunities to form that bond—to fall in love with your child. As you take care of and care for your child, bonding can occur in many little ways.

Self-esteem depends on *unconditional* love: love with no strings attached; love with respect, acceptance, appreciation, empathy, sensitivity, and warmth; love that says, "Regardless of what you do, I love and accept you for who you are."

A day-care provider told me about two-and-a-half-year-old Joey, who would say when he got in trouble, "That's okay, because my mom and dad still love me!" His parents had laid a solid, loving foundation.

Conditional love, on the other hand, is turned on and off. It manipulates behavior by saying, "I love you *when* ____, *because* ____, or *if* you do something." Kids who receive only conditional love never really *feel* loved; when they receive love they can't trust it. These kids try to *earn* love by becoming people pleasers.

Children have their own life force, their own opinions, dreams, and destinies. The challenge of parenting is to allow and encourage children to be themselves while guiding, supporting, and celebrating their process of growth. Successful parents not only love their children unconditionally, but also protect them, set limits, and assume as much responsibility as is necessary for the children's age and developmental stage. This constancy of love and protection is crucial—even in the event of separation or divorce of the parents.

Newborn infants are totally dependent on adults for their well-being, but growing children need the freedom to *be* and *act* their age. It's important to turn over responsibility to children as they become ready. If you're helping your child across the street at three, that's great, but if he or she is fifteen, you have a problem. Let your children be silly, let them play, let them be kids while they're kids. The characteristics of children changes with different ages. Knowing this makes it easier for you to work *with* their nature, not *against* it. In other words, "It's easier to ride a horse in the direction it's going!"

The letting-go process is a gradual, orderly transfer of freedom and responsibility from parent to child, from birth to maturity. Through this process, children gain self-confidence, independence, and self-esteem. By the time they are young adults, they will be responsible individuals equipped with the life skills they need to function happily and effectively.

Pause for a moment to reflect on your own self-esteem, as a child and as an adult. Over the years you have had your ups and downs. What were the causes of these fluctuations? Begin to pay attention to the things in your life that have affected your self-esteem.

Low self-esteem comes from

- rejection
- conditional love or no love at all
- lack of attention, being ignored, neglect
- not being taken seriously, not being listened to
- disrespect
- emotional abuse—put-downs, name-calling, ridicule, sarcasm, blaming, humiliation, criticism, threats
- needs not being met
- prejudice
- comparison, perfectionism, always looking for what's wrong
- focusing on externals (appearances, behavior, performance)
- expectations that are too high or too low
- guilt, shame, resentment
- physical and sexual abuse or exploitation

Remember that when children experience treatment of this nature, they conclude, "I'm not important." "I can't do things right." "I'm not good enough." "I'm not okay." If they accept this as their Truth, it damages their self-esteem and puts them at risk.

On the other hand, **high self-esteem** comes from

- acceptance, respect, love
- attention and care
- being taken seriously and listened to
- a feeling of belonging, bonding, having a support system
- honesty (with tact and sensitivity), integrity
- having needs taken seriously and met
- honoring uniqueness
- authentic expression of feelings
- encouragement, support, appreciation, belief in
- safety, security
- being trustworthy, trusting others
- high standards and attainable expectations
- competence, success, achievement
- doing good and being good
- a sense of personal power, having choices
- pride in one's cultural heritage
- personal and social responsibility
- being healthy and fit
- affectionate and appropriate touch
- forgiveness, allowing and learning from mistakes
- having meaning in life, a sense of purpose
- living up to one's own moral standards
- a sense of connection with a Higher Power (spirituality)
- gratitude
- a sense of humor; laughter and play

As your children observe and experience these positive influences in their lives, they conclude: "I'm okay." "I'm glad to be me."

"Mom and Dad think I'm important; I must matter." "I'm worth-while." "I'm loved." Their self-esteem soars.

When you stop doing the things that lower self-esteem and do more of the things that raise self-esteem, you will notice marked improvements in your family relations. Low self-esteem cannot be "fixed." Over time, however, you can help it to heal.

One day I realized that when I'm using low self-esteem be-haviors—criticizing, blaming, yelling—my kids feel bad, *and so do I*. On the other hand, when I'm using high self-esteem be-haviors, *everyone's* self-esteem increases! When I'm good to them, we all come out winning! When I'm nasty, we all suffer. For better or worse, self-esteem is contagious. Families with high self-esteem are a lot more fun!

The essence of self-esteem is compassion for yourself and for your children. With compassion you understand and accept yourself. When you make a mistake you forgive yourself. And you do the same for your kids.

Needs vs. Problems

Plants need good soil, water, and sunshine to flourish. To thrive, children also need optimal growing conditions. First and foremost, they need unconditional love. They also need to feel safe at home and at school; they need to know they will not be harmed. They need to feel secure about the future and not con-stantly worry about what is going to happen. It is the job of the family to meet the needs of children. If children's needs are not met, there will be problems.

If you ignore the needs of your houseplants—soil, water, sunshine—your plants might die. If your car needs maintenance and you don't fix it, you'll obviously have car trouble! If your house needs roof repair and you don't take care of it, you'll be in trouble with the next downpour. Either we tend to needs or we have problems.

Children (and adults) have basic physical needs: They must have shelter and food to eat. They also have emotional needs that must be met: love and respect, acceptance and understanding, support and encouragement, affection and belonging, and security (which comes from structure, freedom, and predictability). Meeting these needs will ensure their physical and emotional well-being. They will thrive. Ignore them and you (and your children) will have problems. Tending to the basics when children are young can prevent pain, grief, and expensive therapy when they are older. An ounce of prevention is worth (at least) a pound of cure.

Families that do not meet the basic needs of their members are dysfunctional families. The persons society labels "sick," according to the late Abraham Maslow, have never had their basic human needs met—or they had at one time, then lost that basic need satisfaction to some trauma or another.

What is the best medicine then? "For a child who hasn't been loved enough," wrote Maslow, "obviously the treatment of first choice is to love him . . . , just slop it all over him. Clinical and general human experience is that it works." This also holds true for adults. The same things that build high self-esteem in the first place can heal the damage later on.

If your emotional development was stunted as a kid, there's hope! Healing is possible when you take care of your needs, fill in your developmental "holes," and become whole. As you build a solid foundation of love and protection for your children, you also do it for yourself.

Self-Esteem Game

Get a partner to play this with you. Sit facing each other. One person, A, looks the other, B, in the eyes and says, "Tell me how you're terrific!" That's the only thing that A says.

B responds by saying, "I'm terrific because ____," and then

completes the sentence. B repeats this sentence with different endings for three or four minutes. At the end of this time you switch roles.

After you have both taken a turn, talk about it. How did it feel to hear those terrific things about your partner? How did it feel to say those terrific things about yourself? Exciting? Unusual? Uncomfortable?

Almost everybody enjoys listening to the wonderful things happening in the life of a partner. In fact, many report that just hearing all the good news affects their self-esteem. Many people get embarrassed because they haven't thought of themselves in terms of "terrificness." Many are uncomfortable because they don't value what they do in the "line of duty." Many feel as if they're bragging. Yet Will Rogers said, "If it's the truth, it can't be bragging." And remember, "terrific" does not mean "better than."

Helen, a grandmother attending a workshop, shared her insight after the exercise: "I got in touch with my roots—with who I really am. I went back to the joy of the little girl I used to be—before I was contaminated with the negative messages of growing up."

So "flip" your focus from negative to positive. Start catching yourself—and your kids—at being terrific. You are terrific—and so are they. *Whatever you look for, you find.* Talk them about their qualities and strengths. Catch them being good and reward them with your attention. It is especially important to handicapped children that their abilities are emphasized, not their disabilities. Positive thoughts are a beginning, just as a basket of flower seeds is a beginning. The next step, however, is to plant those seeds in their hearts so they can blossom. They need more appreciation. Give it to them. *What you focus on expands.*

Look also for the strengths in your family. Too often people focus on the weaknesses and take positive qualities for granted.

They need an attitude adjustment. Talk about your family strengths, then give each other appreciation and hugs. A family is sacred. A lot of esteem is built into creating a secure and nurturing home for the people we love.

3

Self-Esteem
Protection Skills

"No one can make you feel inferior without your consent."[1]

Eleanor Roosevelt

The bumper sticker on the blue sports car in front of me reads, "If you're cute, honk. If you're not, bark." The put-down startles me. This is but one small example of the cruelty people inflict so carelessly on strangers, acquaintances, and members of their own families. Negativity is so common that it seems normal in our culture. Like pollution, it creeps into our homes and under our skin. We have to be aware of toxic levels in our environment and our systems lest our self-esteem be damaged.

As children we learn quickly that the world can be full of downers. School days are filled with chances for humiliation. Typical self-esteem eaters kids encounter daily are: being put down by peers, called names, embarrassed by teachers, and abused by bullies; wearing the wrong clothes, getting poor grades, dropping the ball in PE, and forgetting important things at home; awkwardness around the opposite sex, not knowing where they belong, and not understanding what's being asked of them.

Hopefully, by the time we've reached adulthood we've begun to learn how to keep these things from sending our self-esteem into a tailspin.

Everyone—children and adults alike—needs strategies for *increasing* self-esteem and strategies for *protecting* self-esteem from bullies and toxic people and situations. One of the most important things you can do in your daily life is to keep self-esteem high— and one of the most important things you can do for your kids is to teach them how to protect and nurture their own high self-esteem. Self-esteem carries its own momentum—the more you have, the less time you need to spend putting the pieces back together.

Think of a time when your self-esteem was really high and someone flung an insult your way. In your confidence you let it go right past, thinking they didn't know what they were talking about. The better you feel about yourself, the less vulnerable you are to negativity. Now remember a time when your self-esteem was sagging and someone gave you a compliment. You may have denied it or found yourself looking between the lines for "what they really meant."

If someone offered you a plate of garbage, would you say, "No thanks" and go on your way? Or would you take it anyway because you don't know how to say no?

Without self-esteem protection skills, many reach for food, alchohol, drugs, or other substances and behaviors to soothe the discomfort and pain. With new skills you can set boundaries and teach others how to treat you well. Here are some strategies both you and your children can use for dealing with daily slings and arrows.

- **Inquire.** Asking, "Is something wrong?" or "What do you mean by that?" throws the responsibility back on the insult giver and invites them to talk about it. Perhaps there was some miscommunication.

- **Confront.** You don't need to grin and bear it or be a martyr. If a put-down hurts you, you might say "Ouch" or "I don't like that." Children can also use the "snake sound"—hissing at the person and pointing two fingers like the tongue of a threatened, dangerous snake. This may be easier for kids than defending themselves verbally.
- **Outlaw put-downs.** This is a technique used by teachers. They teach children to be alert to attacks on their own self-esteem and that of fellow students.
- **Withdraw.** We don't want to be around people who are nasty, cruel, or annoying. This can be a lifesaver in some cases. But be careful—don't overuse this one.
- **Don't take it personally.** Mostly kids and other people do things for themselves, not against you. Maybe they're having a bad day. Maybe they're unaware or simply careless. The put-down probably has nothing to do with you. Instead of reacting, you might find out what's underneath the barb.
- **Humor.** As the shortest kid in his class, José was sometimes called "Shrimp." He'd look them right in the eyes, smile, and say, "Hmm, I love shrimp."
- **Make a neutral remark.** When they finish, say, "Oh," or, "I see." Leave it at that.
- **Consider the source.** Some people seem to wallow in negativity. Let them express whatever emotions they choose, knowing they have little or nothing to do with the real you. Consider, for example, the person who calls someone else a "nigger"; this insult reflects *their* prejudice and narrow mindedness.
- **Disagree.** Realize that what people say is just their opinion; you know yourself better than they do. You might disagree or say, "You're entitled to your own opinion."
- **Sift through.** Perhaps there is some truth in what they're

saying but they haven't yet learned good, gentle feedback skills.

- **Call a friend.** A shoulder to cry on can comfort and strengthen you.
- **Use positive self-talk.** Repeat over and over to yourself, "No matter what you say or do to me, I am a worthwhile person."[2] Teach these strategies to your kids and to anyone you know who is in a toxic or abusive situation. It will help to protect the inner core of their confidence and self-worth.

Here are some strategies that have worked for other people.

- **"Wax your back."** A dear friend of mine once told me that every morning he waxes his back and his life is great. No, it isn't to rid himself of superfluous hair, it's a metaphor to protect him from whatever negativity might "rain" on him in the business world, just as oily feathers protect a duck. He takes preventive measures to safeguard his self-esteem.
- **Duck.** In Arab lore, people supposedly "dodge curses" as if they were avoiding physical objects being thrown at them. You can do this mentally, too.
- **Wear a shield.** In your mind, wrap yourself in white light, or an invisible bubble of protection. Any negativity that comes your way cannot penetrate to wound you.

- **Give yourself a hug.** Give one to your kid. Hugs are great as a send-off in the morning, a welcome home later on, or an affectionate good-night. Life is better with hugs!
- **Clothing and jewelry.** Wonder Woman has bracelets and a "golden girdle." People wear "power" clothes when they want to make a good impression—when, for example, they want to borrow money from a bank. A piece of jewelry or a special garment, (maybe Batman underwear!) can give a sense of personal strength and power.
- **Permission to be different.** Kids (and adults!) often get a lot of pressure to be like everyone else. They get teased because they are wearing the "wrong" clothes. If you teach them that they are unique and don't have to act and dress like everyone else, they'll be less affected by those pressures. Give them permission to be different— to be who they really are.

You don't have to put up with put-downs. You don't have to be a toxic waste dump. You don't have to give others the power to hurt you. Try these strategies—or others of your own—until you find some that work for you, that help you maintain your self-esteem. And teach them to your children.

These skills can be crucial for children who have characteristics which bring more attention to them, such as a hearing aid or prosthetic. Children who feel good about their unique differences are more tease resistant. Role play to practice self-esteem protection strategies and responses; model the positive language they can use in these situations. You may discover some interesting things. A child who has a wheelchair may become aware that he or she is an expert at using it, and can do things other kids can't. One mother, when she learned that her young daughter would have to wear glasses, began to call her "my beautiful four eyes" in a loving tone of voice. Later on, when kids teased her, she didn't even recognize the intended insult!

You will not and should not always be there to protect your children. Help them learn how to protect themselves.

You need to know when to put your defenses up and when to let them down. Seek out people who are safe to be around, who you can trust. Help your kids do the same and increase the *positive* energy in this world! Help them learn to put insults where they belong—in the trash!

"If there is no enemy within, the enemy without can do you no harm."[3]

Old African Proverb

4

"I Know They Love Me, But I Don't Feel It."

"The remarkable thing is that we really love our neighbor as ourselves: we do unto others as we do unto ourselves. We hate others when we hate ourselves. We are tolerant toward others when we tolerate ourselves. We forgive others when we forgive ourselves. It is not love of self but hatred of self which is at the root of the troubles that afflict our world."[1]

Eric Hoffer

On their twenty-fifth wedding anniversary, a wife told her husband that she had been showing her love all those years by warming his plates for him. He replied, "I hate having warm plates!" Apparently they then were able to work through this miscommunication because they went on to celebrate their thirtieth anniversary . . . probably with cold plates.

There are two parts to communication: sending a message and receiving it. Most parents probably love their children, but because of personal shortcomings and faulty communication styles, children do not feel loved. Their self-esteem suffers needlessly.

In my workshops I ask parents how many *knew* while growing up that they were loved by their parents; many hands usually go up. Then I ask how many *felt* loved; fewer hands are raised.

Sometimes parents who really love their children don't know how to express that love; sometimes the children don't know how to accept it. A parent of a teenage bulimic confessed, "My daughter never felt loved, but I love her very much!" Being loved does not necessarily mean feeling loved. Yet feeling loved is the first and most fundamental need of a child.

In our society, many men are taught from childhood not to express their feelings, and consequently deny them. Those who learn to block out difficult emotions have a hard time finding access to beautiful feelings of love. Shere Hite's survey of seven thousand men revealed that almost none of them were close to their fathers. Raising children was often considered "women's work," and fathers, working away from home for long hours, had little contact with their kids.

Another survey revealed that fathers spend an average of thirty-seven seconds a day interacting with their infants. Other research showed a marked decrease in contact after a divorce: by early adolescence, 50 percent of the children from divorced families had *no* contact with their dads, 30 percent had *sporadic* contact, and only 20 percent saw their fathers *once* a week or more.[2] Yet children need their dads as well as their moms, regardless of whether they are living together or living apart. They need to connect deeply—emotionally—with them. They need to hear "I love you" and *feel* loved by them. And dads need to love and feel loved by their children.

What did you get from your father? What did you *want* from him? What you wanted is probably what your children need and want from you.

If you did not learn to love as a child, now is the time. Kids are perfect to start on. They're receptive and responsive, and can teach you what love is. Learn to receive love, to love yourself. Then you can more easily nurture, love, and parent your children.

> *"If we cannot love ourselves,* where will we draw
> our love for anyone else?"[3]
>
> *Mildred Newman and Bernard Berkowitz*

What *Does Not* Communicate Love

Much harm has been done in the name of love. Parents with good intentions try to show their love in many ways that don't work, such as the following:

- **Overpermissiveness.** Parents think, "My kids know that I love them because I let them do anything they want to." A high school friend of mine who could stay out as late as she wished came to the conclusion that her parents didn't care enough to set a curfew. Children need safe, healthy, and reasonable limits; our willingness to set those limits conveys love.
- **Martyrdom.** Many women are taught self-sacrifice—continually giving to others without taking care of themselves. They set aside their own needs, believing this is the way to express love for their families. Many end up as martyrs and doormats. By putting themselves last, they eventually feel resentful and depleted, and their children do not feel loved. It is important for parents to take care of themselves, to see to their own needs. Then they will have more to give to those they love. Some parents do too much for their children—things

that children should be doing for themselves (including solving problems). They deprive the children of the opportunity to learn, gain confidence, and build their self-esteem. These children come to expect that someone else will always "do it for them." We empower children by encouraging them to think and do things themselves.

- **Overprotection.** In this sometimes scary world we live in, our children need to be protected from danger and harm. However, if we overprotect them, they conclude that they aren't capable. If you're holding your kid's hand as you cross the street and your kid is sixteen . . . well, you might want to look at that.

- **Material possessions.** Linda, a thirty-six-year-old mom, told me, "My father would buy me anything I wanted, but he would never hug me or show me any affection. I've spent my whole life feeling that he didn't love me." She felt indulged but not loved. Instead of presents, give your children your presence. (If you buy less you can work fewer hours.) *The best thing to spend on your children is your time.*

- **Quantity time without quality.** Spending lots of time together does not necessarily communicate love. Many people raised by adults who were with them twenty-four hours a day felt unloved. Kids need a great deal of our time for daily attention and care. With new skills, parents can increase the quality and mutual enjoyment of that time together.

- **Conditions.** Some parents say, "I love you when ____," "I love you if ____," "I love you because ____," or "I love you but ____." Strings attached to love cast long shadows. Conditional love is a manipulation or maneuver to improve performance; it doesn't convey love. Remember, "I love you" is a complete sentence.

What *Does* Communicate Love

Larry, an older man attending a workshop, said, "I felt loved when my dad carried me on his shoulders and sang to me." One woman felt loved when the family built an ice rink and then went skating together. The love in their families increased, as did the self-esteem. Those endearing memories came from having fun.

Take a few moments and ask yourself what situations made you feel loved as a child. Are you doing things like that for or with your children?

There are many ways we can communicate love effectively to children.

- **Being with, not doing for.** It's easy to get caught up in always doing things for children. It's important, at times, to put aside all the busyness and just be there with them.

This is especially true in times of crisis. When children (and others) feel this quality of presence, they conclude, "It's important for you to be with me. I must matter. I am loved." Their self-esteem goes up—and so does yours.

- **Taking them seriously.** The things that happen in your children's lives are of tremendous importance to them. Put yourself in their shoes and value what they share with you.
- **Really listening.** This is one of the most basic and important life skills and will be discussed in the next chapter.

How can we communicate to children that they are worthwhile and valuable?

- **Nonverbal messages.** Positive facial expressions, eye contact, loving touch, and attentiveness make others feel important.
- **Positive words.** Everyone wants to hear good things about themselves. Make sure your words are sincere.
- **Respect and enjoyment.** Children read our attitudes. When we have fun with them, everybody wins.

An Exercise in Self-Care

Our emotional state can change faster than the weather. It goes up and down according to the interactions with ourselves and with others. Like a checking account, we can feel full one day and overdrawn the next. We need to monitor these feelings closely, keeping ourselves out of debt—out of emotional pits—as best we can.

Children and parents alike need love, support, and nourishment. When your life is concerned with caring for others, *self*-care is essential. If you're running on empty, you have nothing to give. So it's very important to learn how to increase deposits and fill yourself up.

You deserve to have fun, to enjoy life. It's okay to do the things you want to do. You deserve to be happy. When you are good to yourself, you feel good about yourself. As your home becomes more nurturing for you, it also becomes nourishing for your children.

Here is a favorite exercise in self-nourishment. Make a list of twenty things you love to do. Some are things you'd do alone, some with your children, some with your spouse, partner, or friend. Then cross off any that are not good for you. Be aware, as you are writing, of when you last did those things.

Your homework: Every day do at least one of those things for yourself. Be good to yourself. You deserve it!

Take very good care of yourself, because your children are counting on you to take good care of them!

> "If everyone had just one single person in his life to say, 'I will love you no matter what. I will love you if you are stupid, if you slip and fall on your face, if you do the wrong thing, if you make mistakes, if you behave like a human being—I will love you no matter,' then we'd never end up in mental institutions."[4]
>
> *Leo Buscaglia*

5

Listening Skills

"To the depth that I am willing to reveal myself to you, to that depth can I know myself."[1]

John Powell

Kids who grew up under the children-should-be-seen-and-not-heard rule had a distinct handicap. They were deprived of the opportunity to express their thoughts and opinions and to gain confidence in their own abilities. Many of them came to believe that what they had to say wasn't important, that they weren't important, or even that no one cared about them. Their self-esteem suffered.

The first time I felt really listened to, I was about seventeen years old. I spent the night at my friend Annie's home. She and I talked and talked into the early morning. Annie cared about what I had to say and really listened to me! I felt surprise, relief, joy, and closeness. Really listening expresses interest and caring. It is a powerful and intimate experience that enhances self-esteem and friendship.

Remember a time when you had something very important to say but the person you were talking to was not listening well; the listener either wasn't interested or didn't know how to listen;

or perhaps it was just a bad time to bring up that particular subject. What was that like for you? What did you feel?

Now remember a time when you had something to say and *were* listened to. Chances are you felt that you were being "taken seriously." You felt important, and your self-esteem went up a few notches. For effective listening, we need to listen to others as we would like them to listen to us.

Some people feel rejected, angry, unimportant, worthless, or unloved when they're not heard; they may want to close off or withdraw. Carl Jung once said that people are in institutions because no one would listen to their stories.

Communication skills are the most basic, important skills that we need in life. Without them we are doomed to continual frustration, misunderstandings, and loneliness. Since the intrusion of television into family time—when people sit back passively and ignore each other—communication patterns have changed dramatically, and many vital skills have been lost. Wendy Sarkissian, an Australian social planner who conducted extensive research in the suburbs of New South Wales, stated, "My view is that whole generations of women are being lost to us. . . . I've talked to women who've lived for four and a half years across the street from other women and have never even introduced themselves because they seem to have lost the skills of getting to know people, the skills of operating comfortably with other women or with other people."[2] Communication skills allow us to develop friendships and deep love relationships that enrich our lives and enhance our families.

A friend recently returned from a two-month stay in a village in northern Thailand where there was no electricity or telephone service. Every evening the family built a fire outside the home and sat around it talking with each other for about two hours. Everyone in that culture naturally learns to tell stories and to listen. Having no written language, the transmission of their cultural history depends on the people's communication skills.

Listening skills are not difficult to learn. Once you learn to use them and teach them to others, they will transform your relationships and raise self-esteem.

- **Be interested. Look interested.** Look into the eyes of the speaker. (When listening to children, sit or crouch down to be at their level.) Face the speaker directly; if you are both sitting, lean forward slightly. Actions speak louder than words. Let your body say, "I'm interested!"
- **Put aside judgment and criticism.** Get into their experience and feelings; get inside their shoes and try to understand what happened. Put yourself and your own concerns aside. Don't think about what you'll say next.
- **Be aware of nonverbal cues.** Note the speed and inflection of the voice; the sighs and gulps; posture; the eyes glazing over or tearing. Reading between the lines gives you important information.
- **Let them finish.** Don't interrupt. While you are the listener, let the speaker do the talking. At times it may be okay to briefly interject something if it enhances the other's story. It's also fair to ask them to repeat a point you're not clear on. Remember, however, that the speaker has the ball; do not take it away. This may be difficult for those who are used to communicating competitively—impatiently waiting for a comma, then jumping in. Give them the kind of attention that you enjoy. It's a gift that says, "I care about you," "You are important to me." You'll get your turn afterward.

If you have actively listened, you have gathered much information. You noticed body language; you probably figured out the feelings involved—you know what you would have felt if this had happened to you.

- **Reflect the feeling(s)** back to the other person, from his or her point of view. For example, "I'll bet you were scared," or "You must have been really excited," or "You must feel ____ because ____."[3] This direct response to them about their experience completes the transaction.

If you reflected accurately, the speaker will probably breathe a sigh of relief at being understood or perhaps will exclaim excitedly, "Yes, that's right!" If you have not reflected accurately, the speaker has an opportunity to clear the misunderstanding. The need for a response is so important that little children may repeat a statement over and over and over again until the parent comments. The response lets them know that they were heard. The transaction is complete.

The conversation can then take one of several turns. The listener can help the speaker explore the situation ("Would you do it that way again?") or offer guidance ("How can I help you?"). Then the listener can speak, expanding upon that topic or telling another story.

Like a tennis match, good communication involves give and take. Taking turns is only fair. It is essential for mutual satisfaction and enjoyment. Interrupting, on the other hand, is annoying and not fair play, unless it is short and to the point, and relevant to the speaker's train of thought. Some people are skilled interrupters who take the speaker's story and run with it, effectively creating a power play that damages communication.

Some speakers tend to derail and wander off the topic. Both speaker and listener should pay attention to tracking and also to the deeper issues.

Practice active listening with someone. Find a time that is convenient for both. Read this section together, then take turns being the speaker and the listener, each talking for about two or three minutes. Afterward, discuss how it felt. Did you really feel listened to? If not, what might your partner have done differently so that you would feel listened to? Give feedback in a positive way; for example, "When I noticed your arms were folded, I thought you weren't interested in what I had to say. I would appreciate it if you didn't fold your arms when you listen to me."

If, as the speaker, you were really listened to, you probably experienced some or all of these feelings: excitement, interest, a sense of closeness to the listener, validation, self-worth, understanding, love. As a listener you probably felt interest, trust, enrichment from a new experience, excitement, and closeness to the speaker. You have given a great gift. Self-esteem on both sides has increased. This is win-win communication.

Think back to the time when you felt that you weren't being heard. Who came out winning? No one.

Good listening skills are no more difficult to learn than driving a car. They need to be practiced. At first they may feel awkward and artificial. That's okay. Keep at it, and they'll get easier. After a while they will be automatic. Like driving, it becomes second nature—and is just as effective for getting from place to place!

A good time and place to practice listening skills in a family is at the dinner table. To even out participation you can have a talking stick (or a spoon), which grants the bearer the right to be listened to. When he or she finishes, the stick is passed along to the next person who has something to share. In one family, every Friday night was "free speech" night. Family members could say anything they wanted without fear of consequences. It was a special time for airing problems and building understanding within their family.

Good listeners take the time to listen. They take breaks from the business of life just to *be with* those they care about the most. They help people discover that they have stories to tell. Good listening keeps people healthy and happy. It's an important skill that will improve the quality of your family life, your relationships, and everyone's self-esteem. As the saying goes, "There's a reason that we have two eyes, two ears, and only one mouth."

> "If you take time to talk together each day,
> you'll never become strangers."[4]
>
> *Leo Buscaglia*

6

Asking and Refusal Skills

"So much to say. And so much not to say! Some things are
better left unsaid. But so many unsaid things can become
a burden."[1]

Virginia Mae Axline

To ride a bicycle, you must know how to make it go and stop,
and how to make it turn. Communication skills are just as basic.
You need sending skills to let others know what you want and
don't want. You need listening skills for understanding, for resolving differences, for closeness, and for love.

There are three basic ways people use to get what they want:
monster ways, mouse ways, and assertive ways.[2]

Monster ways include shouting, venting anger recklessly, hitting, manipulating, and intimidating others. *Mouse ways* include
crying, whining, begging, pouting, hinting, getting sick, and hoping someone will read your mind ("If he really loves me, he'll
know what I want!" works only if he or she is psychic). Monster
and mouse communication styles may work, but they usually
create bad feelings in the process. Remember a time when you
yelled or cried all day, then got what you wanted? Was there any
sweetness in getting it?

Stereotypically, males are taught an aggressive (pushy) communication style, and females are taught a passive (pushover) communication style. Then, traditionally, we take one of each, put them together, and tell them to live happily ever after!

The best way to communicate is *assertively.* This involves knowing what you want and then asking or telling others: "Would you help me?" "I don't like it when you ___." "I'd really like to get together more often." "Please give me a hug."

Instead of complaining about how hard you work, for example, and how ungrateful everyone is, say, "I worked very hard today and would like some applause, appreciation, flowers, or hugs." When we ask for what we want, we are much more likely to get it; unlike mouse and monster communication styles, asking does not cause residual negativity. Do remember, though, to be sensitive to the timing of the question/request.

Asking questions when you don't know or understand something leads you out of confusion. It is not a sign of weakness or failure, but a powerful tool for helping you get your needs met and increasing your sense of self. Sometimes it's hard to know what you want, so pay attention to your feelings. Follow your anger to its roots. Listen to your fears and their message. Tune in to your desires and wishes.

Asking may feel strange at first, but it will get easier. Asking for what you want and need takes practice. It can be difficult or intimidating at first, but it is worth the risk. Openness leads to honesty, which can be very rewarding.

It's okay to get what you want. Allow yourself to receive. You deserve it. Let others help you. This in turn can give you the strength to help others.

We can ask questions to express interest and caring for others. Open-ended questions ("Would you tell me about your day?") encourage more talking than questions that can be answered with one word or a phrase ("How are you?" "Fine."). To improve communication, ask, "How do you feel about ____?" "What do you want?" "How can I help?" Asking in a respectful tone of voice can lead to greater understanding.

Teaching children to ask empowers them to get their needs met. Young children who know how to ask for a glass of water, for example, don't have to whine or cry or act out in other undesirable ways to get their thirst quenched. Direct asking can make life much easier for parents. You don't have to try to read their minds.

Children—and later, adults—who have special physical or mental challenges need to learn to feel comfortable asking for what they want and need. A friend of mine who works with special-needs children has found that those who can assert themselves and make their needs known have the best chance of reaching their full potential. For example, a hearing-impaired child who is "mainstreamed" in public school classes may have to ask to sit up front or ask the teacher to face her or him as much as possible; he or she may even have to ask the teacher to wear an auditory microphone that transmits sound directly to the hearing aid. Other children may need to request extra teaching time or tutoring. Once they are aware of special needs, most schools are good at providing support. Since few teachers are mind readers, a hearing-impaired student may need to request these things. If children are timid or embarrassed or afraid of being different, their needs may not be met.

In general, asking directly is easier with people who know how to say no. When communicating with people who can't or won't say no, we have to second-guess them and make assumptions about what we think will make them happy, about what they will or will not like.

Everyone needs to be able to say no. As adults, "no" lets us set limits for our children and ourselves. It helps us maintain integrity. As youngsters, children need to learn that their bodies belong to them alone and that they have the right to say no to anyone who might try to touch them. Older children need to learn to say no to drugs, alcohol, and promiscuous sex. If they have not been taught refusal skills, children will be vulnerable to pressure and manipulation, to pitfalls and dangers.

Saying no, like braking on a bicycle, defines our boundaries—how far we will go, where we draw the line. Saying no keeps us from biting off more then we can chew. It helps us to be in the driver's seat, and can help decrease stress by caring more for ourselves. Saying no lets us stop what we don't want and get more of what we do want. "It is not okay to say no, however," writes author Patricia Palmer, "if it is a responsibility or something you have agreed to do. And remember, how you say no makes a difference. Treat others as you like to be treated."[3]

Many people have great difficulty saying no. If this is a problem for you, complete this sentence several times: "Saying no means _____." Allow yourself to become aware of why it is difficult for you to say no.

One of the reasons people have difficulty saying no is that they have negative associations with the word. Perhaps you find this true of yourself. For many people, saying no means rejection, selfishness, guilt, failure, weakness, stubbornness, hurting other people's feelings, not being liked by others, risking anger . . . No wonder saying no can be such a no-no!

Now think of the *value* of saying no.[4] Write your thoughts down before reading further.

Saying no is like giving yourself a present—of honesty, freedom (you don't feel used), relief, authority, peace, power, confidence, and integrity. It establishes boundaries. It gives you self-definition and self-respect. It gives you time and control over your own life. It makes your yeses more meaningful. Parents have to say no many times, until a child develops the judgement skills and ability to say no for themselves.

Sometimes parents threaten their kids saying, for example, "If you don't stop that, I'm going to spank you." A much better word choice to stop unacceptable behavior is a simple, firm "No," or, "Stop that." As parents we must say no when our child's health or safety is at risk. Like anything else, however, "no" can be overused, rendering it ineffective (like the boy who cried wolf). Say yes at least three times more often than you say no. When you say no, sound serious; lower the tone of your voice. Look serious; a smile may confuse them. Say no with respect and firmness. Avoid being nasty. *You don't have to be mean to mean business.*

One summer, for example, my sixteen-year-old son Felix told me he wanted to learn skydiving with his friends. I could have lost my cool. I laughed (probably out of nervousness), then joked about it ("Well, Felix, do you have insurance?"). Then I firmly said, "No, you may not do it. I love you and want to enjoy you for many more years to come." He and his buddies went to the airport to watch what was going on, and after seeing the setup, realized that he didn't even want to do it.

Kids need to explore the world and learn about life. Guide them in this process of discovery while keeping in mind their age and developmental needs. Toddlers, for example, need to touch. Instead of saying no all the time to my first two babies (born eleven months apart!), I put my special things out of reach and allowed them to touch other objects with only one finger. This satisfied their need to reach out and explore without the risk of destruction.

Women face additional difficulty in saying no because of the myth that "when she says no she really means yes." When women say no, men may not take them seriously, and thereby disempower them. Certainly many cases of date rape have resulted from this communication tangle. If saying no is very difficult for you, consider going to a therapist or an assertiveness class. The ability to say no and mean it is the source of much personal power.

People who talk and listen to others can form and maintain healthy, happy relationships. They can share ideas, opinions, and feelings without fearing judgment and criticism. Learning and practicing communication skills increases understanding, trust, openness, closeness, and love between people—and everyone's self-esteem goes up.

7

Dealing with Feelings

"It is terribly amusing how many different climates of feeling
I can go through in one day."[1]

Anne Morrow Lindbergh

Everyone is born with a full deck of capabilities—physical, intel-
lectual, spiritual, and emotional. We need to learn to play them
well in order to become healthy, fully functioning individuals.

Often, though, there are some
cards—some aspects of ourselves—that we don't know how
to deal with. In our society we
learn that certain feelings are
appropriate and fitting for
males, others for females. But
emotions are neither masculine
nor feminine; emotions are
human. We need to experience
a full range of feelings to be fully
human. When this does not
happen, we unconsciously may
pass on our own emotional

limitations to our children. Even so, children must learn to deal with all of their feelings if they are to live their own lives fully and freely.

What kinds of feelings did your parents express? How did they express them? What did they do with other feelings? Whose pattern do you tend to follow?

"Say you're sorry!" "Tell me you love me." "You should be happy." "Don't be mad." "You don't really feel that way." It's easy to try to force feelings on others. When parents dictate or manipulate kids' feelings, though, they pressure them to give up their own emotional reality. Kids cannot do this; they can't manufacture emotions. With you-shouldn't-feel-how-you-feel messages, kids conclude that their feelings are unacceptable, wrong, or even nonexistent. They conclude that they can't trust others with their feelings or, perhaps, that they can't trust their own feelings. Robbed of feelings, they lose their grounding in reality.

Not knowing what to do with their emotions, children hide them—from themselves and others—or deny them altogether. They may become isolated in fear, worry, embarrassment, anger, or guilt. They may build protective barriers around themselves that eventually increase their isolation. They may repress their true feelings while pretending to feel differently. Or as they create defenses to protect their true feelings, they may come to identify with those defenses rather than their own emotions. Later on they may habitually turn to alcohol and other drugs to manage or completely numb more difficult emotions.

"Safety disappears when you decide what children 'should' enjoy"—or feel. "Respect for separateness proves you care," writes author Dorothy Corkille Briggs. Everyone has a right to his or her own feelings. And this right must be accepted and protected. Kids have their own bodies, their own minds, their own dreams, and their own feelings. They are unique individuals, different from you. "Your way of seeing and feeling is not the only way of seeing and feeling," writes Briggs.[2]

It can be hard to accept children's feelings—especially if we have trouble accepting our own. Yet children can teach us *how* to deal with feelings! When children hurt themselves, they cry and shriek as though their whole world has fallen apart; a few minutes later, once the problem is addressed, they're laughing. Healthy kids emote all the time; they roar and cry and yell and giggle and keep their emotions *in motion*, moving through them. There are no mixed messages or double meanings here. Their words (or other noises) and body language clearly let you (and everyone else!) know their emotional state at the moment. Like the weather, when the storm is spent, the sun shines again, and all's well with the world.

Getting comfortable with your feelings can help you reparent yourself as you parent your child. When you accept children's emotions—whatever they may be—you help them to "own" their feelings. They conclude, "My feelings are okay, even when they're not the same as my dad's," "It's okay to be me," "I'm okay." Self-esteem goes up when you honor differences.

Feelings are valid; respect them. Feelings are our guides through the human experience; listen to them. Pay attention to the subtleties of tenderness, sorrow, reverence, joy. Honor them. Take a deep breath. When we have feelings we can't handle, we hold our breath. When we breathe through them, we release them. Inhale. Exhale. Repeat. Feelings that have been "stuffed" for a long time may become distorted and exaggerated. Accept them. Allow them to be. They are okay. Allow yourself to feel the pain, the anger, even the hatred that might be inside. Acknowledging these feelings is the first step toward releasing and resolving them.

Understanding your *emotions* can help you *feel* better. "Feelings seem inappropriate only when they are not understood," states author Claudia Black.[3] *All feelings are okay.* What you do with your feelings—your behavior—can be judged as acceptable or unacceptable.

If you share your feelings openly, children and others understand you more and don't have to rely on guesswork to know what's happening. In expressing feelings you might say, "I feel mad/glad/sad because ____," and then ask for what you want. Talking things out can release internal pressures, help you gain perspective, and open you to the support and caring of others. Not talking about your feelings can create anxiety, tension, and distance. *You teach your children how to handle their feelings by how you handle yours.* One of the most important jobs of parenting is to notice, label, and affirm feelings.

When children get hurt, encourage them to say, "Ow!" If a physician is giving a shot and it hurts, saying "Ouch!" can help release the pain. The more it hurts, the harder they should yell. This lets others know how they feel. Encourage them to ask for what they want (a kiss, perhaps, or a Band-Aid).

My friend Laurel recently wrote, "The other day my two-and-one-half-year-old, Amanda, was screaming with anger when my husband left the house in a hurry one morning. Baby Patrick was screaming at the same time. I wanted to scream, too! But I got Patrick to my breast and calmed Amanda enough to listen. I said to her, 'You're angry because daddy left and didn't say goodbye to you. Is that right?' Suddenly she stopped sobbing, and looked at me in surprise, then nodded furiously. 'I no know daddy is gone,' she said. The next minute she became her calm and focused self again!"[4] Sometimes just setting words to an emotion lets us understand it without having to "act it out."

When we repress feelings tension builds up in our bodies. This pressure may be turned against the self, in the form of psychosomatic or psychological problems, or it may be directed against others in the family or in society. Yet we need to use care in expressing them so we don't harm our children. Laurel wanted to scream, but controlled the impulse. Identifying the feelings can help us to get some distance from them.

Feelings are private, internal experiences that tell us about our world, that help us make decisions and form values. They are normal, natural responses to experiences. We can react, knee-jerk fashion, to our every feeling, letting them run our lives, or we can be in charge of our emotions and decide if, when, and how to respond to them. We need to teach our children how to act appropriately on their feelings.

Feelings can also follow our thoughts (self-talk). Fearful thoughts, for example, lead to feelings of fear, which lead to a certain set of behaviors. If, while walking home at night, I worry about getting mugged, my body tenses; my breath gets shallow; expecting trouble, I walk faster, I get home tense and nervous. If, on the other hand, I'm thinking about how happy I'll be to get home and see my kids, I feel happy; I breathe deeply, I am aware of the world around me and friendly to others. Thoughts and feelings affect almost all decisions, no matter how mundane.

When your child wants an ice cream cone, for example, and you cannot or do not want to buy one, you could

- deny your child's feelings ("You don't really want an ice cream cone")
- manipulate his or her feelings ("You shouldn't feel that way before dinner")

Or you could

- accept and acknowledge the feelings ("You'd sure like to get a cone right now"), then
- intervene at the thought level ("But it's too close to dinner time and it would spoil your appetite"), or
- intervene at the behavior level ("Sorry, we can't get one right now, honey"), or even
- intervene with the imagination ("I wish I could buy you a triple-decker. What flavors would you have?")

Our culture does not affirm feelings; it is generally not safe to express them. We need to know when to reveal our emotions, and when to keep them in check. We need to be able to be real, to be who we are at home. You might say to your child, "If you want to talk, I'll listen; if you want to be alone, I'll understand."

A journal is a wonderful tool for sorting through confusion, for releasing tension, for learning to deal with emotions. This evening, list the emotions you felt during the day. When did you feel them? Where in your body did you experience them? How did you express them? Did they remind you of anything? What feelings were missing? As you clarify your feelings, you can identify patterns in your emotional processes that will help you to change and grow. A journal can start you on the path to becoming your own best friend.

Trust

"I think we may safely trust a good deal
more than we do."[5]

Henry David Thoreau

A child wonders: "Is this world a friendly, safe place for me?" "Can I depend on being fed when I'm hungry, on being comforted when I am hurt or frightened?" "Are my needs being fulfilled?" "Can I count on my parents?" "Can I be myself?" The child either concludes: "I can trust" or "I cannot trust."

Trust has been defined as an act of faith, belief in another, confidence, predictability, the absence of fear, a willingness to be vulnerable, feeling safe, the basis for intimacy. For trust to develop, children must feel safe. Parents must create a safe environment for their children. In creating safety, parents lay the foundation for trust and health. The young people, a survey shows, who are most vulnerable to peer pressure are those who distrust messages they receive from the significant adults in their lives.[6]

"The single most important ingredient in a nurturing relationship—in any relationship—is honesty," states author Claudia Black. No one can trust, or be expected to trust, unless people openly and honestly talk about what's important and about their feelings. Dishonesty creates confusion and destroys trust. If you do not tell the truth, neither will your kids. They learn from you. Children want honesty. Let's resurrect the old saying, "Honesty is the best policy."

This doesn't mean, though, that you have to say everything that's on your mind. A classmate once told me: "My parents encouraged us to say anything we wanted to each other. But we had to be careful how we said it." She learned early in life how to be truthful, sensitive, and tactful.

When a baby is born, parents often start playing mom and dad roles. They become less of who they really are, and more of who they think they're supposed to be according to the models and myths of parenthood they've learned. Yet, when parents aren't being genuine human beings, children find it difficult to know them or trust them.

> "In a very serious way, this transformation is unfortunate because it so often results in parents forgetting they are still humans with human faults, persons with personal limitations, real persons with real feelings. Forgetting the reality of their own humanness . . . , they frequently cease to be human."[7]
>
> *T. Gordon*

The same holds true when parents maintain a facade of perfectionism, for example—when the appearence of being a "perfect" family has a higher priority than having loving, solid relationships within one. Unrealistic or impossible expectations breed disappointment and distrust (see Chapter 19).

Distrust can result from disrespect, fear, neglect, insensitivity, ridicule, humiliation, rejection, neglect, and abuse. Trust must be reasonably and consciously cultivated. I used to think that trust was like being pregnant—all or nothing, with no in-between. Then I learned differently. We can't trust anyone 100 percent of the time. Using good judgment, we must figure out how far and in what situations we can trust people. At what age can you trust your child to carry a cup of water? When are they old enough to cross the street by themselves? When are they ready to babysit? The art of parenting and our wisdom come into play with day-to-day decisions.

Kids need to be able to trust their parents. And parents need to be able to trust their kids. Who do we trust? We trust people who are worthy of trust. We must be trustworthy for our kids.

We can build trust with our children in a variety of ways.

- Treat them with respect and caring.
- Accept them for who they are. Honor differences.
- Meet their needs. Feed them when they're hungry; see that they get enough sleep. Help them feel safe.
- Spend comfortable, quality time together. Be there for them.
- Comfort them when they're afraid. Hold them when they're hurting.
- Avoid unpleasant surprises and punishments. Learn non-damaging discipline (see Chapter 13). Create a familiar, predictable, comfortable routine.
- Don't make promises you won't keep. If you won't do it, don't tell them you will. Maintain your own integrity by being accountable to them.
- Say what you mean—using tact—and mean what you say. Don't give insincere or undeserved praise.
- Respect their boundaries, their privacy. Don't force them to say things they don't mean.
- Let them know they can count on you. Tell them when and where you are going and when you'll return.

- Prepare them in advance for big events in their lives. Let them know what to expect.[8]

Sometimes trust begins with a leap of faith on the part of the parents—a gift of respect, of believing in their children. It's important to set high (but attainable) standards for your children, and live up to them yourself. Wanting to live up to your expectations, kids become trustworthy. For this reason, we have an obligation to trust them so that they can become trustworthy. We need to focus on their strong points, build on them, encourage them to be their best.

An eighteen-year-old girl told her parents that their greatest gift to her was their trust. Her peers would stay out late or do something unacceptable, knowing they would be yelled at, grounded, or lose driving privileges. Katie's parents' trust was a strong deterrent, because she didn't want to lose it. She could be honest with them because she had trust in them, as well. By being trust*worthy*, she learned to trust herself.

Parents also need to learn to trust themselves more, thereby modeling trustworthiness. A trusting environment is one in which safety and honesty, connectedness and love, can flourish. Relationships in families call for the greatest possible amount of trust.

Guilt and Shame

Guilt has been defined as moral self-disapproval. It is a feeling we have when we know we've done something wrong. In fact, there are many levels of guilt, ranging from embarrassment to shame. The dictionary defines guilt as "the fact of being responsible for an offense or wrongdoing." It is a specific state of being that can be removed by making amends. Yet when wrongs are not righted, guilt becomes a burden; it can destroy self-esteem and cripple lives with anxiety. It can turn into a sense of shame, which the dictionary defines as "a painful emotion caused by a strong sense of guilt, unworthiness, or disgrace." To shame is to bring dishonor or disgrace.[9]

The origins of our shame often precede our birth and are imbedded in our society. For myself, a good little Catholic girl, the concept of "original sin"—that mysterious, indelible mark of evil on my soul—devastated me and continually undermined my self-esteem. Though I had done nothing wrong, I grew up suffering a bitter, undefined, unnameable shame. According to John Bradshaw, shame is one of the major destructive forces in all human life.

A general sense of guilt occurs when persons do not have a self-defined set of values and moral standards, but subscribe unconsciously to a "secondhand" value system. Values come from parents, significant others, schools, churches, and other social institutions. Cultural values are reflected in the language itself. Values that are defined by others can set up a dissonance within ourselves; we want to do what we are "supposed" to do, but we often fail.

Our culture can give us many sources of shame: being poor; being disabled; being a person of color or from a foreign country; having alcoholism, incest, or other dysfunction in one's family; not fitting into accepted gender role definitions; being homosexual or bisexual. The list goes on and on. In this way we can even feel guilty about things for which we are not responsible.

Some parents, for example, feel guilty about a child's "handicap," as if it was, in some way, their own fault. If you carry around this type of guilt, acknowledge it and realize that it is normal to feel this way. Talking about it will reduce the discomfort and anxiety. It will help you not to pass those feelings on to the child, who has to live with the handicap. Then let this guilt go. It gets in the way of how you view your child, and later how the child will view him or herself, and you. It keeps you from acknowledging the facts. Become comfortable talking about the handicap, and your child's self-esteem will go up. Disclosure to others goes a long way toward minimizing a child's chance of rejection by his or her peers.[10]

The family can also be a breeding ground for guilt and shame. Living in close proximity and having emotional bonds with other people requires a high degree of accountability and interpersonal responsibility. Adults often use guilt to manipulate others in order to get what they want. Mothers and Jewish grandmothers have a bad rap for this. The problem stems from the lack of skills for communicating directly. Asking for what you want requires a sense of self-esteem and confidence. When guilt is used to manipulate, disappointment can be blamed on others. Blaming and shaming create a cycle that is hard to break.

When children are manipulated by guilt, they learn to shame themselves. Philip Oliver-Diaz and Patricia O'Gorman write in their book, *12 Steps to Self-Parenting*, "Unfortunately, in most addicted families, shaming and humiliation are the chief tools used for controlling children."[11] When parents are shame based and lack self-esteem, they cannot give love to themselves or others; they cannot model healthy ways to express feelings, set boundaries, be intimate, or solve problems. They do not know these things themselves and therefore cannot teach them to others. Their children are deprived of the bottom-line basics in life and carry the shame into yet another generation.

In a family of guiltmongers, there is little sense of unconditional love. Objects and affections that are ostensibly gifts from the heart end up with strings attached. Parents keep kids off balance with statements and accusations. "Shame on you!" "How could you do this to me?" "You're trying to undermine me, aren't you?" "How dare you?!" Blanket statements like "You always _____" and "You never _____" instill in children a deep sense of shame and unworthiness, even if they are only slightly negative.

One forty-eight-year-old woman stated, "I wasted my childhood tormented with guilt and fear. I tried so hard to be good, yet I always felt bad. I tried to second-guess my mom all the time so I could avoid being blamed and criticized. I was a good little girl who grew up paralyzed by fear and guilt. If, driving down the street, I'd see a policeman, I'd feel an intense wave of anxiety, even though I had done nothing wrong!"

Specific guilt is a healthy thing, a feeling that tells us when something is wrong. It refers to one specific reproachful action. It's okay for children and adults alike to feel bad about doing a bad thing. Sorrow or remorse are appropriate. Feeling the pain lets you take responsibility for your part of it and make necessary changes. The desired outcome is to fix the mistake, learn from it, move on, and not repeat it. Finally, forgiveness heals and completes it. The child (or adult) thinks, "I did a bad/stupid thing, but I am a good person and I can correct my mistakes."

For someone who carries around a great deal of general guilt, absolution can be a difficult task. Here are some ways you can begin to work through and unburden yourself of guilt.

- Minimize it. Break it down. Ask yourself, what one specific action is the cause of the feelings of guilt?
- Find the source. Who or what was judging your behavior?
- Separate yourself from that source.
- Ask yourself, deep inside, what you believe, want, and choose for yourself.
- Correct the guilt-producing behavior. Make amends.
- Listen to your self-talk. You talk yourself into feeling guilty; you can also talk yourself out of it.
- Know that you are okay. You always did the best you could given the information you had at the time.
- Forgive yourself and let it go.
- Realize that what you did is not who you are.

Shame is intensified by secrecy. It's hard to identify shame, because it lurks beneath the surface and speaks to us in disguised voices. Moving beyond shame is not as easy as fixing a mistake. Amends are harder, perhaps impossible, to make. And yet shame must be healed before growth can take root.

- Name and acknowledge the shame.
- Talk about it. Breaking the silence can help release its grip.
- Give yourself the gift of total acceptance—moles and warts and all.
- Again, find the judge. Acknowledge that this voice may simply be wrong.
- Affirm that you are not perfect, but are okay and worthwhile.
- Choose to love and embrace yourself unconditionally just the way you are.
- Determine your own values and live by them.

The more you sift through and unravel the knots of shame, the less likely you will be to pass it on to your children.

Grief

"Good Grief!"

Charlie Brown

Grief is our body's way of responding to and moving beyond loss. Grieving is a growth process that is misunderstood and neglected. When we don't know how to deal with it, we get stuck in the loss and pain.

My Uncle Franz lived with my family for many years. This arrangement started with my parents' marriage; he even went with them on their honeymoon in my father's Essex! His relationship with us ended with his death when I was 14 years old. During my childhood, he had been the love of my life, my best friend and confidante within the family. His death devastated me. My parents didn't know how to handle their own grief, or anyone else's. At the funeral I spoke out of turn and was slapped. I was punished for acting out my grief. Life went back to normal as quickly as possible, and we rarely mentioned him around the house. It just wasn't practical.

Twenty-five years later I confronted my loss. A therapist suggested a memorial service. So I set aside a full day for the mourning. I draped a large box with black velvet, burned incense, and looked through old photo albums. I remembered him and talked to him and cried; I visited a mortuary, a cemetery, a church, moving through and beyond the loss and pain that had gripped me for most of my life. I finally put him—and my deep wound of grief—to rest. I finally said "goodbye."

Every child, every adult, experiences numerous losses. They may include illness, moving, disability, divorce, death, abandonment, abortion or miscarriage, children leaving home, retirement, fire, war, and dealing with addictions. We are ill-prepared to deal with our own losses, and have great difficulty dealing with those of our children. As parents we want to protect them from life's painful realities, and yet we lack the skills for dealing with such heavy things. We have a tendency to

- deny or bury our feelings. "Big boys don't cry." "Don't feel bad." "Get hold of yourself."
- replace the loss. "We'll get you another bike/pet/friend."
- grieve alone. We don't trust others with our tears and pain.
- just give it time. "Time heals all wounds."
- change the subject. We pretend we have our pain under control.
- intellectualize. "Be thankful you have another friend," or

"We know how you must feel."
• keep busy. We try to forget.

"All of this bad information causes massive pain," write John James and Frank Cherry in *The Grief Recovery Handbook*.[12] Beginning at birth and ending at death, loss punctuates our life. New skills, journal writing, therapy, and support groups can help us complete our own grief recovery.

In helping little ones to deal with and heal their little losses, we can learn new skills for dealing with big ones. For starters, extra attention is required to reduce stress and to nurture the healing. During the hard times of loss, set aside special time *just to be there* with the other person. Comfort them. Hold them. Put yourself in their shoes. Invite them to talk. Listen to them.

"What happened?"
"How did you find out?"
"Would you tell me about it?"
"I am sorry!"

Kids are transparent. You will know when the storm has passed and the grieving is complete. Likewise, your own life changes when you have recovered from your own grief.

Anger

"Don't hold onto anger, hurt, or pain.
They steal energy and keep you from love."[13]

Leo Buscaglia

Eight-year-old Andy hits his little sister. His parent yells, "Stop that! Say you're sorry. Give her a big hug." Those orders ignore and deny Andy's feelings and demand hypocritical behavior; he's not sorry and he doesn't feel like hugging her!

Here's another approach: Stop the behavior. ("You may not hit your sister!") Then realize that the behavior came from a feeling and a thought. He's hitting for a reason; he's angry about something. Accept his anger and help him turn his feelings into words. ("You're mad. What's going on?") Get into his shoes and understand what has happened from his point of view. *Talking it out prevents acting it out.*

Channel the angry feelings into neutral or positive actions: "When you're angry, you can pound the pillows on your bed or hit the punching bag. You may not hit your sister." Andy concludes, "My feelings are okay. And I'm okay. It's not okay to hit my sister." He learns clear boundaries and some healthy ideas for dealing with his anger in the future. Another five-year-old has diabetes, which triggers big feelings of anger and frustration. She has a blow-up clown as a punching bag that she can hit, instead of hitting other people.

In our culture, when little girls get mad, they quickly learn that it's not okay: Nice girls don't get mad; however, it is okay to be hurt. On the other hand, when little boys get hurt, when a pet dies, for example, they quickly learn that boys don't cry. It's not okay to hurt; it is okay to get mad. For many people, emotions have been cross-wired. Women, when confronting someone in anger, may burst into tears; men suffering pain and loss may punch someone out. Anger, pain, joy, and love are not male or female feelings; they are human emotions felt by everyone.

Anger is a normal feeling. It identifies a problem needing a solution. We must accept it in our children as well as in ourselves. By expressing anger we and our children learn how to handle it. When we learn to express it in a "clean," nondamaging way, it is easier to accept—in ourselves and in others.

If we were abused as children, we had destructive, violent examples of how to be angry. We must now learn constructive ways to express anger, so that we don't end up hitting, or exploding, or making ourselves sick by turning the anger inward.

A good thing to do when you're angry is to buy time. Say to your kids, "I'm feeling angry and I need to be alone for a few minutes so I don't take it out on you. We'll deal with this later." Then get away and do something to help you restore your reason—physical exercise, a shower, a phone call, a good cry, writing about it. Going off by yourself can give you a different perspective. Time out will help you to regain your balance and perspective, as well as show them how to effectively deal with anger.

If the intensity of your anger is out of proportion to the situation, call time out to focus on what you "triggered." Get off by yourself so you can figure it out. Write about it in a notebook or journal. What happened? Why? What else was going on? What's underneath it? Once you unravel it, you defuse the trigger. One mother told her therapist that she "lost it" when her baby cried. Delving into this problem, they discovered she had a deep-seated belief that if her baby cried, it meant she was a bad mother. Understanding this, she could grapple with her beliefs, and modify her feelings and behavior.

Like other emotions, anger is short lived. Research shows that the "anger reflex" lasts only about one second. Anger comes mixed with other feelings—fear, frustration, and love. Take, for example, the situation of a child getting lost in a store. Mother probably feels anger, fear, love, and relief when the pair are reunited; the common response, however, is to express only anger to the child. A healthier and more honest response would be to talk about the anger, then about the fear, the love—and the relief. Try this "Total Truth Process."[14]

- Express the anger: "I'm angry that you wandered off."
- Express the pain and fear: "I was afraid that something bad might happen to you that would hurt you."

- Apologize: "I'm sorry that I was taking so long looking for shirts."
- Express desires: "What I want is for you to stay close enough to see me so I know you're okay. I want you to be safe and content. Maybe if I bring along some books or toys next time it will be more fun for you."
- Express love, forgiveness, appreciation: "I am so glad you are okay! I love you so much and don't want anything bad to happen to you." Hug and comfort the frightened child.

Many people get "stuck" in the anger, the pain, or the fear. Express one feeling, then move on to another until all the feelings are addressed and released. This is an amazing process. At first do this in letter form with no intention of sending it; this is for you—to release and heal your anger and pain. Start every section with "I." Try writing this "love letter" to get out of the anger and get back to the love. Once the negative feelings are released, the bottom line is, "I love you."

Here are other tools for dealing with anger.

- Deal with your anger as you would like others to deal with theirs.
- Learn to release anger without harming yourself or others. Rule out emotional or physical violence.
- Use inanimate objects if you have to hit something.
- Bite your tongue, if you have to, to avoid a cruel tirade.
- Keep it short, focusing on one problem only. Then forgive and forget.
- Separate the behavior from the person. Treat the person with respect and deal with the unacceptable behavior.
- Use "I" statements.
- Don't displace anger on innocent people. It's not fair to make your kids suffer because you're angry at your boss.

- Use active listening skills.
- Be honest. Kids can sense your feelings. But you don't have to tell them everything. You can say, "Sweetie, I'm angry right now, but I'm not angry at you. It's my problem and I'm working it out." Be truthful but not cruel.
- End on a positive note.
- If your anger is dangerous to you or others, get help.

There is a difference between anger and rage. Anger is momentary and specific. Yet we all have rage, says author Marion Woodman. Rage is an intense, transformative energy that builds on top of past wounds to us, to our ancestors, to all humanity. It is deeply stored, at a cellular level, and can color our temper when it flares up. Woodman suggests working through one's deepest rage with a therapist, to get it all to the surface, or in a group that can help you handle and channel it.

In the absence of support, you might lock yourself in the bedroom and pound pillows to let off steam that would otherwise harm your kids. Adding words to this physical act will intensify the release. I once had a special closet that served the purpose of sanctuary. I would scream in my car, too. It helped me survive the worst of times.

Children often compare themselves to others, then get angry when they are unable to do certain activities as well as they want to. This is particularly true for children with special needs. It is important for children to be given permission to show their feelings. Reflect their feelings back to them: "I can see that you are frustrated when you see other children doing things that are difficult for you. It is okay to show you are feeling that way, because feelings are important."

Frustration is undirected anger We get frustrated when circumstances are beyond our control. When anger is not resolved it can become frustration, and frustration can become resentment.

Resentment

Unfinished business from the past has a way of reappearing. It nags at us demanding our attention and wanting a resolution. Anger and resentment possess us, punish us, and imprison us in the past. They create tension in our lives.

Pay attention to the tension, to the old, nagging anger. Where does it come from? Whose voice do you hear? What did you do? Write about it. Follow it to its root cause. Research shows that writing increases our self-awareness and revitalizes us by putting us in touch with our inner voices. Release from inner tension strengthens our immune systems.

One strategy for letting go of resentment is to write a letter to the person you resent. Take a moment to get in touch with all the feelings you still have concerning this person. Honestly allow those feelings to flow onto the paper without censoring them, because you really have no intention of mailing this letter. This one's for you. If the "old" pain reappears, write another letter. You may need to pound pillows, talk it out with a trusted friend, or find a therapist to help you deal with difficult emotions. The next and absolutely crucial step is to forgive yourself for having had "negative" feelings toward another and toward yourself.

Few parents intend to be cruel. Few people mean to be unfair. "If they don't mean it," you might ask, "why did they do it?" We may have been wounded in the past because

- they may have thought that we deserved it. "This hurts me more than it hurts you," we heard as they inflicted punishment.
- they may have had poor impulse control. Drunk or enraged, they may have unfairly hurt us. They hadn't yet learned responsibility for their own feelings and behaviors.

- their personal struggles may have spilled over onto the innocent. We may have been in the wrong place at the wrong time, for example, been caught in the crossfire between Mom and Dad.
- they may have made mistakes and hurt us, even though they had good intentions. They may have bungled a situation while trying to do their best. A depressed person, for example—with intentions of lightening the burden of others—may take his life, creating a great deal of pain for his family and loved ones.[15]

Resentment has a price. Pain denied and stuffed into the unconscious never loses its power; the wound does not heal. Are you tired of dragging such feelings around with you through life? Are you willing to let those who hurt you off the hook? When we face the pain squarely, we can let go of the past and move ahead with our lives. Forgiveness, of ourselves and others, dissolves the tension and releases old pain.

Forgiveness

People are not perfect. We have all been hurt by the mistakes of parents, teachers, and other important adults in our lives. Blame and resentment trap us in the past—a past that is ancient history and has no place haunting and interfering with present life. Forgiveness releases us from that past and lets us heal ourselves and our memory. It sets us free from the prison of pain we never deserved.

Forgiveness has a twofold purpose: to heal ourselves and to heal the damaged relationship. My relationship with my mother had been filled with conflict for half a century. Over the years I had worked toward healing and forgiveness, yet we never seemed to understand each other. Finally, I attended a workshop where we did an exercise on forgiveness. The instructor gave me orders to let her off the hook! The next day I visited my 88-year-old mother in her nursing home. I started awkwardly. "Mother, we need to talk." Then, "I've been a difficult child for you, I know." I told her I was sorry for the pain I had caused her. I then told her that she did all right as a parent and that I'm okay, too. With her eyes closed she was fading in and out; I wasn't sure if she had heard me. I went on and thanked her for the good things she had done for me, and listed a few. "I love you," I said, and I meant it fully. Then I paused, feeling complete. I asked her if she had anything she wanted to say to me. After a long pause she said, "Forgive me." Those were her last words to me. She died three days later. Perhaps that's what she was waiting for. I wish it hadn't taken so long for us to make peace.

The process of forgiveness begins with courage—and a decision: the willingness to be honest with yourself, to see more clearly and reframe your thinking. Unravelling faulty thinking can help us begin to heal.

Many people overgeneralize: "This is wrong, that is wrong, therefore, everything is wrong!" They jump from a few specifics to a global catastrophe: "Everything's totally and completely awful." To reverse this process, think of someone who is "all bad." Look for the specific behavior that bothers you; then consider all the other attributes that make up this person. What someone does is not who he or she is.

Separate who people are from what they do. When examining pain, be very specific about harmful incidents. What particular behaviors wounded you?

Forgiveness does not mean approval. It involves a willingness to see with new eyes—to understand and to let go. They did what they did out of their own weakness. You did not deserve it. They could not teach you what they did not know. They could not give you what they did not have.

When you understand that they are not awful people, but

perhaps frail and needy persons who have made painful mistakes, you are moving closer to forgiveness. When you can wish them well, you'll know that forgiveness has begun. As you peel off the layers of old hurt, anger, and guilt, underneath you'll discover a beautiful, loving, more relaxed and capable you.

Examining old wounds, and releasing the anger and pain, ensure that we won't recreate the same wounds in those we love the most. We have all been wounded. Instead of wounding our children, let us heal ourselves.

It doesn't matter your age, or your color,
or whether your parents
loved you or not
(Maybe they wanted to, but couldn't.)
Let that go.
It belongs to the past.
You belong to the NOW.

It doesn't matter what you have been.
The wrong you may have done.
The mistakes you've made.
The people you've hurt.

You are forgiven.
You are accepted.
You are okay.
You are loved—in spite of everything.
So love yourself, and nourish the seed within you.

Celebrate you.
Begin NOW.
Start anew.
Give yourself a new birth today. . . .
Today can be a new beginning, a new thing, a new life![16]

Clyde Reid

Gratitude

"If the only prayer you say in your entire life
is 'Thank you,' that would suffice."[17]

Meister Eckhart

We all have much to be thankful for. In visiting other countries, I notice many people who appear to be poor yet feel rich. In contrast, many Americans appear to be rich yet feel poor. We often don't appreciate how much we have, and instead are anxious about what we don't have.

High-powered television advertising instills in us a gnawing dissatisfaction with what we have and a desire for what we don't have. Under its spell, we begin to think of our wants as needs. We are talked into needing items that we have survived without for many years. No matter how much we have, we are not satisfied. It's never enough. A Russian recently asked an American tourist, "Why do you need ten of everything?" In our culture we absolutely lust after material possessions.

The epidemic of perfectionism fuels this dissatisfaction. Perfectionists are always wanting something they don't have in order to fulfill an ideal image. This results in an orientation to life that precludes deep satisfaction and makes finding true self-esteem difficult.

Gratitude, on the other hand, reduces tension. Focusing on the positive aspects of ourselves, our children, and our parents lowers personal and interpersonal stress. Counting our blessings increases our joy.

A friend of mine pauses before each meal to hold hands around the table with her family and guests and to give thanks— for the food, for each other, for whatever is positive in their lives. Rituals such as this are special times of closeness and appreciation.

Although my mother-in-law lived meagerly, she was grateful every morning simply that she had another day to enjoy, that the birds were singing, that there was food in the refrigerator. Noticing and giving thanks for the "little things" made her life rich.

With gratitude, we focus on what we do have, not on what we don't. Sprinkle your day with "thank you's." Everyone deserves to receive more of them. Appreciation and recognition enhance self-esteem and make family living more fun.

Coping Skills

Emotions can be guides for making necessary and important choices in life. Expressing and accepting responsibility for our feelings is easier for people whose parents accepted their feelings when they were small.

If you have difficulty expressing your feelings, a very good friend, counselor, or support group may be able to help you release the backlog and learn healthier ways to deal with them. Don't keep emotions to yourself. Find a way to share them; take the risk. If you don't deal with them, they'll deal with you! Here are some ideas for coping with your feelings.[18]

When you are feeling:	And you're tempted to:	Choose a more helpful way to cope:
Nervous	Smoke	Make a list of your strengths
Angry	Lose your temper	
Lonely	Get in trouble	Get physical exercise
Wild	Overeat	Talk out your feelings
Disappointed	Turn to drugs or alcohol	Take a walk
Bored		Do relaxation exercises
Tired	Stop eating	Ask for help
Down on yourself	Destroy something	Write a letter to a friend
Hurt	Make people angry	Do something that makes you feel really good
Cheated	Drive too fast	
Discouraged	Spend money	
	Worry so much you lose sleep	Cook
	Get in a fight	Make music
	Quit trying	Dance
	Avoid the problem	Draw or paint
	Skip a meal	Play sports
	Give up	Clean out a drawer or straighten your room
	Sulk	Count to ten or perhaps a thousand
		Get "involved"
		Read
		Write out how you feel
		Plan something to look forward to
		Rest

8

The Power of Words

"Healthy families remind each other of their goodness;
unhealthy families remind each other of their failings."[1]

Matthew Fox

About twelve years ago while on a picnic in the mountains, my
oldest son Damian asked, "Mom, can I climb that mountain?" I
gave him my okay and off he went. A little later my youngest
son (about seven) asked, "Mom, can I climb that mountain?" "No,
you're too clumsy," I responded without thinking. When I heard
what I'd said, I wished I could eat my words, but it was too late.

Back home, Felix began to drop, spill, bump into, and fall
over everything. He was probably saying to himself, "That important, all-knowing person who is my mother says that I'm clumsy;
therefore I must be clumsy." It was a self-fulfilling prophecy. He
became a walking disaster. Every time he went to pour milk, it
was all over the counter. Knowing I was responsible for creating
this monster, I was careful not to make an issue out of it; I simply
encouraged him to clean it up. After about two weeks he finally
returned to "normal." This experience was my initiation into
understanding the power of words.

Since that time, I have learned how to undo clumsy words.

At the moment I recognized my error, I could have undone the harm immediately by telling my son, "Felix, that was a clumsy thing I said, and I'm sorry," and given him a hug. Then I could have called out to Damian to take Felix along as he climbed the mountain, or I might have climbed with him myself. Somehow, I could have taken his request more seriously.

The language parents and teachers choose and the way they use it can determine a child's destiny. Words have the power to lift up or to put down. With our word choices we build or shred self-esteem.

The words that damage self-esteem are uttered without respect for others. They are spoken in a nasty tone of voice, and can be condescending or cruel. Sometimes as parents, when we feel we are not being heard, we "turn up the volume" in hopes of improving listening ability on the other end. More often than not, though, these strategies are counterproductive. They help turn people—especially kids—into losers. If your parents spoke to you this way, start listening to your own words and to the tone of your voice. Think about who it was that said those things to you. Remember how you felt hearing them and how those words shaped your behavior. Those old patterns may still be operating in your life.

Fortunately, once you have awareness, you have a choice. You can choose to "go on automatic," to do to your kids what was done to you (even though you hated it), or you can choose to become the kind of parent you would like to have had. You can *react*, knee-jerk fashion, and put your kids down, and you will probably regret it later. Or you can choose to *respond*, instead, with care and wisdom.

When you next catch yourself about to react, stop! Bite your tongue if you have to. Take three deep belly-breaths and some time out. If you wait sixty seconds, you can collect yourself enough to respond without hurting your child; if you don't, you'll react from your own childhood and will probably regret it later. Pause to evaluate your thoughts and feelings, and the consequences of possible actions. Think of the positive outcome you want to accomplish and how to bring that about. When you respond, others tend to listen and cooperate. When you react, others tend also to react.

Listen to the words coming out of your mouth. What effect do they have on others? What effect do they have on you? Do you really want to do/say those things? Someone told me once that they never gossip. To them that means they would never say something behind someone's back that they wouldn't say to their faces. This applies to your kids and to other adults. Particularly, don't bad-mouth the other parent to your kids, especially if you are separated or divorced.

Many times we need to bite our tongues to stop a nasty statement from slipping out. In fact, a bit of scar tissue on the tip of the tongue could be a badge of honor. It means we cared enough to stop, take time to cool off, and talk about the problem later when we could describe what we were feeling and what we wanted.

Living in a family requires us to interact with and respond to others. We can do this negatively with criticism or positively with feedback.

Self-Esteem Shredders

Killer statements are most damaging. They should never be used. Examples are

"Don't be you."
"You make me sick."
"You were a mistake."
"I'm going to leave you!"
"I wish you had been a boy/girl."
"I wish you had never been born."
"If I didn't have you, I could have had a career."

Killer statements are deadly—psychologically and physically. Don't ever use them. Other behaviors that convey the same damaging messages are constant ignoring, rejection, battering/ abuse, and acting or speaking as if the child were not there when he or she is there. The latter happens often to severely handicapped children.

Crooked communication sounds positive at first, but has a negative, damaging twist (like "left-handed compliments"). Like greeting cards that look cute and funny on the outside yet are cutting and hurtful on the inside, such statements are often sarcastic, insincere, or patronizing. An occasional sarcastic joke to another adult is one thing, but beware of statements your child might take seriously.

> "You're pretty good at math—for a girl."
> "Oh, you *never* make a mistake."
> "You *always* know the answer, don't you, smarty pants?"

Crooked communication is confusing and painful; it erodes self-esteem.

Negative ways of dealing with negative behavior[2] include criticism, put-downs, ridicule, name calling, blaming, and rejection. "You statements" are common ("You can't do anything right." "What's wrong with you?" "How could you be so stupid?" "You always get into trouble." "When are you going to grow up?"). They are usually delivered in a nasty tone of voice and are often exaggerated ("You always ____" or "You never ____"). Related to external force (and punishment), you statements attack the whole person.

You statements focus on *who you are* (things you can't change) rather on *what you do* (things that can be changed). They point out what is *not* wanted, instead of talking about what *is* wanted. They focus on the past, which can't be changed. "You were late yesterday; you were late last week; in fact, you were *born late!*"

Many of us were raised on you statements. Take a moment and return to your childhood. Do you remember times when people spoke to you that way? What did they say to you? How did they say it? What did you feel about yourself? About them? What conclusions did you draw? How did those incidents affect your relationship with the person(s) involved?

You statements mostly feel like attacks, and when we feel attacked we want to protect and defend ourselves and tune out those painful words. You statements, therefore, can impair our hearing! We cannot understand how the people who claim to love us can hurt us in this way. Instead of being able to respond appropriately, we lock into fear and self-protection, compliance or defiance.

The intent of the parent—to deal with and change behavior—is honorable. The negative methods used to achieve it don't work. You statements don't teach children what it is that you *do* want. Mostly parents don't talk about that. So the child has to second-guess what might please and satisfy the authority figure.

If you tell children they are bad, that's what they believe they are—and that's probably what they will become. Children hear, "I'm no good." "I can't do anything right." "I'm worthless." "I'm not lovable." They draw conclusions, not only about themselves, but also about the parent: "I can't trust you." "You don't care about me." This emotional abuse leads to anger, withdrawal, and rejection. The self-esteem of both parent and child is damaged, and the relationship between the two may be harmed.

It should be noted that not all you statements are damaging; for example, "You did a good job!" "You need to finish putting away the dishes," or "You must be proud of yourself." The tone of voice will usually let them know the type of message you are sending.

If you were brought up hearing negative messages, you have probably caught yourself saying things to your children that you swore you would never say. It is hard to change behavior, especially habitual ways of acting and speaking, but it can be done. It begins with awareness, then a commitment, then working at it. The payoff for you and your children will be tremendous.

Many destructive patterns keep repeating themselves simply because we don't know of better ways to deal with problems. It is crucial that we expand our options. In the days when extended families were the rule and not the exception, there were many role models. We could see how Uncle John played with his kids and how Aunt Judy solved problems with hers. Today, with smaller families, we may be unaware of many options available to us because we have never seen them. Here are some of the positive options that are open to us.

Self-Esteem Builders

Words that build self-esteem are spoken with respect for the other person and with caring about what is going on inside. They are encouraging, and they invite people to become winners. The tone of voice is "clean," not charged with negative emotion. A loving touch—a pat on the back, a hug—often accompanies the words. This is positive feedback.

Positive strokes for being are nourishing and life-giving.[3] Feedback can "feed" the spirit, validate others, and make them want to be winners. Read the following statements and be aware of what feelings they evoke in you.

"You are special and unique."
"You are important to me."
"I like you!"
"I love you."
"I believe in you."
"I'm glad you're here."

Nonverbally these are expressed by an attitude of respect and enjoyment, by affection, by taking children seriously, by spending time with them, and by really listening.

Rewards for doing recognize effort or improvement and show appreciation. Feedback encourages children to do things well.

"Fantastic!"
"Atta girl/boy!"
"It looks like you did your best."
"Keep up the good work."
"Go ahead—try it."
"Look at the progress you've made." (See Appendix A.)

Too many children, and too many husbands and wives, feel unappreciated. Frequent "thank you's" and pats on the back sweeten life and prevent burnout. Give positive strokes not only for accomplishments but also for effort: "Thanks for trying." Everyone needs more appreciation than they're getting. Turn this around. Give others—and yourself—more appreciation than you think is needed. Watch how things change.

Many kids and adults have difficulty with compliments, so they flip one back ("I like yours, too") or shrug it off ("This old thing?"). They don't know what to do with them. It's really very simple. Someone has given you a gift, so just say thank you. If you trust their sincerity, all you have to do is take a deep breath and let it in.

Compliments, like feedback, are more effective when they are descriptive and specific. "I like how you help your brother" gives more useful information than "You're such a wonderful boy." (Hearing "you're wonderful" can also be very nourishing.)

Compliments can feed the spirit in various ways. One dad would put a positive statement in his daughter's bag when he made her lunch; one day he discovered that she had papered the back of her bedroom door with them. In addition to complimenting your child, brag to others; when it gets back to them, it has increased value. And finally, to enhance your own self-esteem, make a list of the wonderful things people have said to you over the years and put in a place where you'll see it often; you can replay these strokes whenever you need a lift.

Respect and caring are keys to dealing with negative behavior positively. We can challenge unacceptable behavior by giving children feedback about its inappropriateness. It's equally important to support and encourage positive behavior and to invite children to become winners.

The underlying message behind feedback is acceptance, valuing, and inspiring the other to be better. It is a strategy for changing others through guidance, encouragement, and support. Feedback can be given as a gift to others out of caring. It is given as a suggestion—something important for others to consider—rather than an order. It works by motivating others to be good, by creating a desire to correct the situation.

As parents we must set reasonable and healthy limits for our children. The most effective way for us to deal with inappropriate behavior is to *separate the behavior from the person*. They are okay, their behavior is not; "I love you, but I do not like what you did!" It's impossible to change who we are, but we can change our behavior.

"I statements" are an effective way of dealing with undesirable behavior. The model is: "I feel ____ when you ____ because ____, and what I want is ____." ("I feel mad when you leave your shoes on the living room floor because they make the room look messy, and what I want is for you to put them under your bed.") I statements are specific, keeping the focus on the behavior, not on the person. They clearly state what it is that you *do* want. With I statements, children learn cause-and-effect relationships (Mom feels ____ because I did ____), and they learn judgment skills.[4]

Another way to deal with negative behavior is with *substitution*.

Stop the behavior you don't want, then encourage the behavior you do want. For example, "Don't do ____; do ____ instead." ("Don't hit your sister; hit a pillow or your punching bag, instead.") Another approach is, "Don't do ____, figure out a better way to do it instead." Every parent has taken a dangerous object from a toddler and replaced it with a toy. With substitution, we stop the undesirable behavior and lead the child to more acceptable behavior.

Feedback, well given, can feel like a gift. There is no need for defensiveness. The child observes the acceptance, respect, and caring and concludes, "Mom/Dad cares about me enough to tell me this and encourage me to be better. I am important. I am worthwhile." The self-esteem of both parties is enhanced. The language and approach allow the receiver to hear what is being said, and the desired change in behavior is more likely to happen.

Observe these two models of critical versus "no-fault" communication:

	CRITICISM	**FEEDBACK**
Leadership style:	Autocratic. Respect may be lacking. Little concern for self-esteem.	Democratic. Based on respect for others. Concern about the relationship; self-esteem.
Based on:	External pressure or force.	Internal motivation.
Underlying message:	You must do things *my way.*	I accept and value you, and encourage you to do better.
Language:	You statements that may be global. "This is how you are."	I statements that are descriptive, specific, and limited to the issue at hand.

Strategies:	Focuses on the person. The whole person is blamed, labeled, put down, rejected. Orders and manipulates. Interactions charged with emotion.	Focuses on behavior. Gives specific information based on personal experience, delivered in a matter-of-fact, friendly, or stern manner.
Response of other:	Feels like an attack; it arouses fear and self-protection, compliance or defiance.	Well delivered, it feels like a gift.
Time frame:	Focuses on past events that cannot be changed, even drawing in situations from years ago.	Deals with the present; focuses on the future, what can be done to improve things.
Outcomes:	Disempowerment, damaged relationship, low self-esteem.	Empowerment, enhanced relationship, high self-esteem.

The "hook" with criticism is that it continues long after the words are spoken. It gets inside and repeats like a broken record. If you pause and listen to your own negative self-talk, you may be able to identify the voices of the important people who, years ago, criticized you ("You're bad." "You're stupid." "You can't do anything right!"). This negative self-talk process can be interrupted and corrected. (See Chapter 18.)

Once you decide to use a better way, you need to break old habits. It's not easy to do, but you can do it. "Turn-about statements" can help. Some people say, "That's the way I am," or "I can't help it if I'm _____," or "I'm the kind of person who _____." Those phrases keep them stuck in the past. Instead say, "I used to criticize my kids a lot, but now I'm learning to give them feedback instead"; or, "In the past I _____, but now I _____." Such turn-about statements can help the transition between how you used to be and who you are becoming.

The next time you hear negative words slip out, stop yourself. Say, "Cancel!" "I'm sorry! I didn't want to say that!" or, "Let me say that differently!" You can engage others in this exciting and heroic process. Talk it over with your kids or spouse. You might say, "I just realized that I've been using the same words that hurt me when I was little and I don't want to do that anymore. The next time you hear me say that, please remind me." Then you can establish a signal like, "Cancel," or, "Replay," or, "Ouch, Dad, try again!" After a while you'll be censoring your hurtful words automatically. Be patient with yourself. Keep encouraging and supporting yourself. Success, it has been said, is picking yourself up one time more than you fall down.

Halting criticism is an extremely important step to building self-esteem. Equally important is increasing the number of positive strokes—appreciation, compliments, and support. A woman in one of my workshops told me that after her oldest children went off to college she paid special attention to her youngest daughter, who suffered from low self-esteem. For two years she focused only on the positive. If she couldn't say anything positive, she said nothing at all. "It worked," she reported proudly. With enhanced self-esteem, the daughter went off to college really ready and confident.

It's never too late to begin. As we decrease the negative attention and increase the positive, we increase satisfaction and joy for the whole family. The Golden Rule of Parenting is: *Do unto your children as you wish your parents had done unto you!*

9

Parenting Responses That Affect Self-Esteem

"Every time I get in trouble you remind me of everything
I've ever done wrong in my life. I'm not too sure what kind
of person I am, but you're convincing me I'm bad."[1]

A junior high school student

For better or worse, adults constantly influence the self-esteem
of children—whether they realize it or not—whether they intend it or not. The words they use fall into four basic types of
responses. Nurturing and Structuring responses increase self-
esteem; Marshmallowing and Criticizing responses tear it
down.[2] Read these examples, and pay attention to how they
affect you.

Situation 1

Twelve-year-old Jennie says, "I want to sleep at Janet's tonight. Her parents won't be there, but her sixteen-year-old
brother will."

Nurturing response:	"You'd like to have fun with your friend tonight. Invite her to come here for the night."
Structuring response:	"No. Unless her parents are home, you may not spend the night there."
Marshmallow response:	"Well, I don't like the idea, but I guess just this one time wouldn't hurt."
Criticizing response:	"No! Of course not! What would people think of us? And don't you know what sixteen-year-old boys are after?"

Situation 2

Judith says, "My husband is away on business, and the baby is driving me up the wall."

Nurturing response:	"You're in a difficult situation, Judith. Ask for help—you need it. The baby needs a mother who is not up the wall. You'll both be better off when you start taking care of yourself."
Structuring response:	"Call someone for help. Find a church or agency that offers child care. Take care of yourself and your baby."
Marshmallow response:	"Poor thing. There just isn't any good help available these days. I hope you make it."

Criticizing response: "If you were a better mother, you wouldn't have that problem!"

Situation 3

Eight-year-old Ryan won't clean his room, and says, "I hate you, Mom."

Nurturing response: "Ryan [touching him], I know you don't want to clean your room and that you're mad at me. That's okay. I still love you. Let's both clean our rooms at the same time, and when we finish, we'll go outside and play."

Structuring response: "We're all part of the family, Ryan, and we all have chores to do. Cleaning your room is an important way of being part of our team."

Marshmallow response: "Don't hate me. You're right, it is too hard for you. I'll do it for you so we can be pals. Maybe when you get bigger you'll be able to do something by yourself, poor thing."

Criticizing response: "You bad boy! Get in your room right now and don't come out until it's perfect! And just wait until your father gets home!"

Nurturing Responses

Based on respect, love, and support, nurturing responses encourage self-responsibility. Parents invite children to get their needs met and offer help in doing so. They believe their kids are winners with the capacity to grow; they give them permission to succeed. I statements and affectionate touch are used.

Structuring Responses

Also based on respect, structuring responses protect, set limits, and demand performance ("I know you can do it!"). Parents expect and encourage children to be capable and responsible. They encourage them to ask for what they need and want, thereby empowering them.

Nurturing and structuring responses work well together. The underlying message for both is, "You are a valuable person. I encourage and promote your growth." The use of these messages results in cooperation, empowerment, win-win situations, and high self-esteem.

Marshmallow Responses

Marshmallowing grants freedom without requiring accountability or responsibility in return. Based on judging children to be weak and inadequate, marshmallow responses disempower while sounding supportive. Blaming other persons, the situation, or fate for a problem, they invite dependence and encourage failure. You statements are commonly used: "Why don't you quit?" "You poor thing, there's nothing you can do." "I'll do it for you."

Oftentimes parents of children who have special needs use marshmallowing responses because they view their child as fragile or less competent. They may feel their child has endured enough punishment in life. These children can develop behavioral problems as a result.

Criticizing Responses

Based on disrespect, criticizing responses encourage children to fail. Ridicule, put-downs, blaming, fault finding, comparing, and labeling are common. You statements are often global: "You always ____" or "You never ____." Humor is cruel; touch is hurtful or punishing. Marshmallowing and criticizing responses are damaging to self-esteem. They result in anger and resentment, in passivity, dependence, and powerlessness.

Changing Response Styles

Which response styles did your parents generally use? Are you glad they treated you that way? Which style do you mostly use? How do you feel about treating your children that way? Many parents find themselves doing to their kids what they swore they'd never do—then feel guilty about it.

It is possible to change your response style! When you let go of the handed-down, damaging behavior, your self-esteem will go up, and so will everyone else's. It's not easy to change habits, but you can do it if you really want to! You will thank yourself a thousand times over; so will your children—and your grandchildren.

One mom yelled at her son, "I'm going to beat you!" Then she stopped herself, realizing that she didn't want to beat him, and added ". . . with a sock . . . with your dad's smelly sock!" She beamed with pride telling her story. In a subsequent letter she wrote: "I'm really excited with the changes in our lives. I really AM becoming the parent I wish I'd had."

Here are some specific strategies for changing from negative to positive response styles.

Change your focus. Instead of always catching your kids being "bad," catch them being good: What you look for, you find. Once you look for the things they're doing right, you'll be surprised at what neat kids they are. Give them lots of encouragement and support ("Good for you!") for positive behavior.

We all need "strokes." People prefer to get positive feedback, but they'd rather get negative attention than nothing at all (being ignored). So focus on and encourage the qualities and behaviors you want.

Expect the best. Kids want to live up to our expectations—unless those expectations are unrealistic or impossible. Expectations of perfection lead to disappointment and despair. Marshmallowing and criticizing parents expect the worst—and they get it! Nurturing and structuring parents have high standards that they communicate simply and clearly; they then encourage, support, and coach their children toward accomplishing them.

Do you believe that kids are worthless and a bother? If so, you will expect that, look for that, and get that. If, on the other hand, you believe that kids are valuable resources who have lots of potential, you will expect, look for, and get that.

Give up blaming and fault finding. Criticizing parents look for what's wrong, find it, then put down their child in order to feel one-up and superior. But no one likes to be put down, ridiculed, humiliated, or blamed. Criticism leads to resentment and anger—or passivity and dependency. It results in powerlessness and discouragement. Everyone's self-esteem suffers.

Nurturing and structuring parents avoid blaming and fault finding; they think, instead, in terms of responsibility. Responsibility means "the ability to respond." Children need to be encouraged to assume responsibility for their behaviors and their consequences. When a mistake is made, it's not the end of the world—it just needs to be fixed. It's easier for children to assume responsibility when they understand that mistakes are opportunities for learning, not for ridicule and shame.

One day, I found a broken jar in the kitchen. I could have yelled and blamed someone. Instead I asked who knew about the breakage. I needed to be sure there was no broken glass to cut bare feet. In questioning my children I found out that it had been broken when my son removed it from the dishwasher; somehow, he hadn't noticed. So together we checked out the machine and removed the remaining broken glass. We both responded to the situation (assumed responsibility for it) and resolved the problem without anyone's self-esteem being damaged.

One of our jobs as parents, is to provide structure (not criticism). We see the results of our parenting responses every day. If we make a commitment to ourselves and to our children to make our responses nurturing and growth producing, they in turn will respond by being better, more responsible people—with higher self-esteem.

10

Parents Are Leaders: Re-Visioning Your Family

"Better one word before than two after."

Welsh Proverb

In families people belong to and with each other in a primal, sacred, undeniable way. Maybe no one has told you this, but as a parent you are a king, a queen, a president. You are an important leader with tremendous power. With this power you can create health, happiness, and high self-esteem in your family, building strong, caring citizens out of your children.

There are five basic components to leadership. Using the example of leading a horse makes them clear.

- **Have vision, direction, goals.** If I am riding a horse, I must know where I am going. The horse does not necessarily know the grand plan, but it is important that I do.
- **Communicate the message.** I must let the horse know what I want by heading it toward the gate. Parents are teachers who must clearly communicate to their children what it is they want.

- **Keep focused.** It's important to keep sight of my vision—I am going out the gate onto the trail. I need to focus on what I *do* want, not on what I don't want. Otherwise we could end up wandering all over the barnyard.
- **Consider needs of others.** Success is more likely if I consider the needs of the horse. If it's very thirsty, I can almost count on having a power struggle unless I allow it to get a drink as we cross a stream. Once the horse gets a drink, we can continue on our way. When people are sensitive to and respectful of each others' needs, they can usually both come out winning.
- **Support the desired progress.** As the horse moves in the desired direction, I encourage and support its progress up and over the hills by talking to it, keeping contact with my legs, and keeping a firm hand on the reins. I give it a pat to reward its efforts. Likewise with children. We don't wait until a toddler speaks clearly in complete sentences to cheer; we get excited about each understandable word and phrase.
- **Expect success and get it.** I fully expect that we will get to where we're going, and we will. Your expectations that your children are healthy and responsible will nudge them along that path.

These components describe proactive leadership. Proactive leaders describe what is wanted in advance and guide the way to it. Most of life's problems can be anticipated and avoided. Proactive leadership (also known as prevention) takes children away from trouble and danger and redirects them to better, safer activities.

The more common style of leadership is reactive. Reactive leadership may seem easier to do (certainly if it has become habitual), yet it actually creates more difficulty and stress. Many parents don't know what they *do* want from their children, and therefore they don't guide or encourage them. An unsuspecting child innocently does something and gets jumped on: "You shouldn't have done that!" The kid is confused and angry because nobody ever told him or her not to do it.

Example: María walks past some toys on the bottom stair; Mom reacts by yelling, "Why didn't you take those upstairs?" The answer is that María wasn't asked to do that, and she's not a mind reader; but she doesn't dare say that. Both parties are angry and María is confused. Anxiety and fear are a way of life.

Reactive parents frequently resort to threats, force, criticism, humiliation, ridicule, and punishment, which create negative feelings both in their children and themselves. Self-esteem plunges. With a little foresight, this can usually be prevented. Parents must clearly communicate what they want in advance. It makes life much easier.

Examples of Leadership Styles

Proactive Leadership	Reactive Leadership
"Childproofs" a home as baby begins to toddle	Changes nothing and constantly says no
Removes broken glass from the yard before a foot is cut	Removes broken glass from the foot
Lets a child know that you must leave in 15 minutes, then perhaps sets a timer for 10 minutes	Waits until it's time to leave, then gets angry because the child is not ready
Tells children you're going to a restaurant and explains desired behavior	Takes unprepared children to a restaurant, then threatens never to take them again
Says to teen, "I hope you'll always let me know where you are and when you'll be back; call if you're late"	Does not discuss plans and expectations in advance, then yells at the teen who arrives home late

Proactive leadership identifies dangers lurking in the world and gives kids permission, encouragement, and support to resist those pressures. I remember Felix commenting that all the billboards in the city were advertising alcohol. I pointed out emphatically how advertising links drugs and alcohol with fun, success, and beauty; we are all being manipulated to want to use painkillers, sleeping pills, and other drugs as a way of life. He entered the "party scene" years with open eyes, and didn't feel compelled to take stupid risks with substances.

The Language of Leadership

Proactive Leadership (Looks toward the future)	**Reactive Leadership** (Focuses on the past)
"That was awful. I know you can do better."	"Why did you ____?"
"Next time, please ____."	"Why didn't you ____?"
"Why don't you try ____?"	"You shouldn't have ____."

Reactive leaders reinforce unwanted behavior by focusing on the past, which we cannot change. Proactive leaders deal with present inappropriate behavior, then lead the child toward improving. ("How can you do it better next time?") They give kids another chance, while guiding and encouraging progress toward the desired behavior. An ounce of foresight is worth a pound of hindsight.

Think, for a moment, about the leadership style of your parents. Was it proactive or reactive? How did it feel to you? How did it affect your self-esteem? What do you want for your children?

Re-Visioning Your Family

In council meetings, Iroquois Indians consider whether their decisions will benefit people for the next seven generations. This long-range vision guides their daily actions and lives.

Vision, direction, and goals are the basis of good leadership. What vision do you have for your family five years from now? In ten years? In twenty years? Keep the vision broad (not "I want my son or daughter to be a doctor"), focusing on qualities and values—not specific goals—that will enhance your lives. Knowing what you want is the first step to getting it. In what ways do you want your family to be like the family you grew up in? How do you want your family to be different? You have the power not only to create a vision but also to live it. You can find and create meaning by clarifying your values. What were the important qualities of the family of your childhood? What was valued? Which of the following characteristics apply to you?

performance • perfection • work • being "good" • possessions
being who you are • adventure • conformity • trust • authority
avoiding conflict • a clean house • friendships • travel
spontaneity • rules • fun • love • choices • acceptance
being obedient • thinking for yourself • openness and honesty
being clean • being pretty • being "nice" • being religious
connectedness • integrity • family unity • taking care of yourself
safety • pleasing others • isolation • keeping down the pain • play
respect • responsibility • self-protection • encouragement
discouragement • risking • taking care of others
belonging • denial • being there for each other

Which of these characteristics led to health and happiness for you and your brothers and sisters? Which did not? Which do you now choose for your own family?

Many years ago I had an important insight. I realized that

if I trusted outside voices more than my inner voice when values clashed, I would be teaching my children values that I didn't believe in and create confusion and conflict (see Chapter 21). For example, I believe that force and violence are wrong, yet my children were learning from other sources that violence was an acceptable way to get what they wanted. I realized that it was important to reexamine and clarify all my values, to pass on those that I truly believed in . . . and discard those that were not really meaningful to me.

Once you have your own vision of a Winning Family, take a small step every day in that direction. Believe in your vision, then communicate it. This can be done in many ways. For example, when my daughter was small, I said to her, "One day you'll be a beautiful, strong woman." To my sons I said, "Someday you'll grow up to be wonderful, gentle men." Without realizing it at the time, I was planting seeds of my vision in my children. Now, as adults, each is sensitive and each is strong.

Talk about your vision. Encourage and listen to their dreams and visions. ("If I could give the world the best present, I'd give _____.") Then inspire, encourage, and support them. Celebrate the little steps of progress.

What is your personal code of ethics? We must teach our children right from wrong. They need basic values and manners in order to get along with others. Teach kindness, respect, and honesty. Teach them the Golden Rule: Do unto others as you would have others do unto you. And do good unto yourself. What we model is what we teach best—and what our children tend to become. If you live your life from your highest values, you will bring peace and compassion to your family, community, and world.

> "Example is not the main thing in influencing others.
> It is the only thing."[1]
>
> *Albert Schweitzer*

11

Parenting Leadership Styles

> "To revere power above everything else
> is to be willing to sacrifice everything else to power."[1]
>
> *Marilyn French*

Were you raised by tyrants? If your home politics were so rigid that strict rules were not balanced with flexibility and freedom, your parents employed an autocratic leadership style—keeping and overusing power. Were you raised by not being raised? Was there too much freedom and flexibility, with no rules for behavior and little guidance when you needed it? If so, your parents were permissive; they relinquished their power or didn't know they had it. Or were you raised by leaders who balanced their power with freedom and caring? If so, your parents shared power in a democratic leadership style. The leadership style parents use reflects their self-esteem and affects the personalities and self-esteem of their children. These styles reflect different uses of power and control—from overpowering to abdicating.

MOST	CONTROL / STRUCTURE / GUIDANCE	LEAST
◄——————————————————————————————————►

| AUTOCRATIC | DEMOCRATIC | PERMISSIVE |

Love is the other dimension of parenting. Love enhances each leadership style, making it healthier for the family. Add love to the autocratic style and it becomes more caring and less damaging. The permissive style without love and support is neglect. Love is the baseline for mental health and successful family life.

After you've identified your parents' leadership style, reflect on how it has affected you. Did you like it? Was it good for you? What kind of a relationship do you now have with your parents? Is that what you want to have with your children when they grow up?

Often children who dislike their parents' style vow that they will bring up their own children differently. Many swing from one extreme to the other, creating a family with just as many problems, only different ones. This swing is commonly from the autocratic to the permissive style.

Autocratic Leadership Style

Characteristics of Parents

Autocratic or "drill-sergeant" parents impose their will through a rigid structure that allows little flexibility or freedom. They tend to

- overuse or abuse power
- impose rigid rules
- take total control and responsibility for all decisions
- take charge of other people's lives without respecting their boundaries
- think that their way is the only right way
- withhold information
- be out of touch with their feelings (or shut them down)
- ignore or put down the opinions and feelings of others ("You're too sensitive" or "You shouldn't feel that way.")

- use pressure and punishment to force compliance
- hurt others

Autocratic parents demand "respect," which sometimes translates as "fear." They tend to believe that children should be seen and not heard, and that a child's will must be broken.

Autocratic parents generally feel

- superior (one-up) and in control
- distrust (or lack of trust)
- burdened with responsibility
- lonely
- low in self-esteem

Characteristics of Children

Placed in a one-down, inferior position to their parents (even when grown), these children work hard at second-guessing, trying to figure out how to please their parents and avoid getting punished. They

- want to be told what to do
- lack a sense of personal responsibility
- may distrust their feelings because they've been told those feelings are "wrong"
- are not creative; lack imagination
- become self-rejecting and lonely
- are compliant and withdrawing (accepting powerlessness) or defiant and rebellious (fighting for power)
- may withdraw by moving or running away

One young mother reported that she had rebelled against her autocratic parents by getting pregnant and keeping her baby in spite of the fact that they wanted her to have an abortion.

Another woman got back at her father by marrying the "wrong" man. (Guess who suffered?) An older woman had dealt with her autocratic parents by moving to Japan. Adolescents who feel their lives are out of control may develop eating disorders to assert control over their own bodies. The autocratic leadership style may work for a period of time, but tends to break down by the time children become teenagers.

In an autocratic family configuration, children tend to feel

- powerless and out of control
- submissive and dependent, or hostile and angry
- distrusting, helpless
- self-rejecting
- lonely, with low self-esteem

These children feel afraid and guilty, yet they don't know what to do with their feelings which are ignored or denied by their parents.

Permissive Leadership Style

Characteristics of Parents

In a very permissive family, there is *too* much freedom. Parents abdicate power. They may be "too busy," alcoholic, ill, or simply disinterested—and the family misses out on the security of rules, limits, and structure. If rules do exist, they are always changing, which results in chaos. Permissive parents tend to

- believe they have no rights
- condone everything their children do
- not be interested in their children or what they do
- be physically or emotionally absent and uninvolved
- neglect their children

These parents often feel

- discouraged
- confused and angry
- powerless and out of control over their lives
- disrespected
- overwhelmed
- low in self-esteem

Characteristics of Children

In permissive families, children

- don't learn boundaries
- have trouble with limits (while at the same time craving them)
- lack self-discipline and responsibility (or may have had to assume too much responsibility too soon)
- may take on an unhealthy role reversal with parents
- are often on their own before they are ready
- think they have the right to do exactly as they wish
- have little awareness of social responsibility
- may become violent toward their parents
- may later seek out highly structured groups, cults, institutions

Children in these families often feel

- powerless and out of control
- unsafe
- unloved
- confused and discouraged
- dependent

- unable to cope with routine
- low in self-esteem

Surrounded by confusion and inconsistency, these children don't feel they can trust their parents.

Democratic Leadership Style

Characteristics of Parents

Democratic families are based on respect. Everyone's needs are considered important. Parents share power with each other and with their children. They offer choices and treat children as capable, worthwhile human beings who are able to think for themselves and make good decisions. They teach responsibility and allow freedom. There may be family meetings involving everyone in making decisions, rules, and plans. There is a balance of power between husband and wife; neither is solely "the boss." Democratic parents

- are in charge of themselves and the family
- provide structure while allowing flexibility and freedom
- give children limited choices appropriate to their age
- invite and encourage children to participate in planning and decision making, yet enforce the rules
- encourage children to learn from mistakes and fix them
- teach responsibility by giving it

Democratic parents function as counselors and coaches. This style—when based on love—is the framework for a winning family.

Democratic parents start from an attitude of cooperation with their children. They

- are in charge, yet flexible
- feel respectful and respected, loving and loved
- trust their children and themselves
- are sensitive to needs
- have high self-esteem

Characteristics of Children

Having a team sense, these children are eager to cooperate. They

- respect rules
- are self-disciplined and responsible
- understand cause-and-effect relationships
- are capable and self-determining

Through making choices and decisions, children of democratic families learn to direct their own lives. They have a friendly relationship with their parents that can someday become a mutual relationship between equals (see Appendix B).

In democratic families, children know they are responsible for themselves and their behavior. They feel

- trusted and respected
- worthwhile and important
- self-confident and self-respecting

They have a high level of self-esteem and a sense of personal power.

A husband and wife attending one of my workshops came to the realization that he was autocratic and she was permissive. The more he swung one way, the more she swung the other. This was confusing to their children and difficult for the whole family.

With this insight into their conflict, this couple had an opportunity to make new choices.

A teenage girl talked about life in her autocratic family: "Often it gets to the point where home seems like a concentration camp, and it becomes a challenge to 'escape.' Tension builds to a disastrous point, with too much emphasis put on chores. People start fighting and hurting each other." She was right. She gave this advice to all parents: "Don't make chores the most critical and important factor in the household. Don't judge kids on their ability to do or concern about chores. Coach and help them without exerting power and forcing them to buckle under your iron will. Try to understand each child's needs, other obligations, physical capabilities, and attention span, and allow reasonable leeway for these considerations. If anger should arise, restrain yourself, and under no circumstances call your children names. Children (including teenagers) are highly susceptible to labels: If you call someone incompetent, he *thinks* he is, and therefore *becomes* incompetent. If you call her stupid, lazy, slow, useless, clumsy, or irresponsible, she is. Kids can be devastated by one careless word thrown in anger. Avoid that anger, and keep your children feeling worthy and confident, making each chore simply a duty, rather than a futile struggle."[2]

Growing up in an autocratic family, it was the only style I knew, and therefore the style that I "naturally" employed with my young family. As they grew and became able to think, communicate, and be more responsible, I found that they were ready and willing to assume more responsibility for themselves, and that I, in turn, could "loosen up." I gradually let go of my need to be in control all the time and learned to share power. In the grocery store, for example, I'd pick out three boxes of acceptable cereal, and let one of my children select one. When they were older, I'd have them read the labels and select the healthiest items. As I trusted them more, they became more trustworthy; as they became more trustworthy, I trusted them more. Shifting from external control and influence to motivation from within, I gradually developed a democratic leadership style. We became a team.

My evolution as a parent was in harmony with the second basic dimension of a healthy family: When children are little, we have complete responsibility for their care and protection. As they grow and develop, we can gradually turn over or share the power and responsibility with them, while guiding and protecting them as necessary.

Democratic parents share power with their children, creating a relationship based on mutual empowerment—instead of mutual victimization. This empowerment is necessary for mental health, for making dreams come true, and for self-esteem in your children and yourself.

In our democratic society, where people must be able to make many decisions, think for themselves, and vote for their leaders, the democratic family is the foundation for these skills, and for a sense of teamwork. As we teach children that they can choose to be who they want to be and do what they want to do with their lives, we are empowering them to build their own cathedrals on a good foundation.

12

Parenting and Empowerment

When you give away some of the light from the candle
by lighting another person's candle,
there isn't less light because you've given some away—there's more.
When everybody grows, there isn't less of anybody,
there's more of—and for—everybody."[1]

Kaleel Jamison

Healthy parenting is nothing if not a process of empowerment. As we help to raise our children's self-esteem, we also increase their personal power. When we encourage them to be confident, self-reliant, self-directed, and responsible individuals, we are giving them power. For better or worse, the patterns of power by which we live, and that our children copy, will profoundly affect their entire lives. As parents, we have much to gain by learning to share power with our children.

As a mom, I taught and encouraged my kids to ride bicycles. There was a rush of pride and power—and a tinge of surprise—as they'd yell back to me, "I'm doing it!" Nearly twenty years after I'd given my oldest son, Damian, one last push on his wobbly two-wheeler, he spent an afternoon looking for the "perfect" bike for me. He taught and encouraged me to use it, giving me that same push back! The icing on the cake came when the whole family had the chance to go touring in Europe—me on my special bike! Each of us was able to push our own pedals and pull our own weight for many days and zillions of kilometers (or so it seemed). It was a satisfying and empowering experience for us all.

My youngest son, Felix, has taught me things I would never have learned on my own. When I'd ask him to fix something for me, he'd show me how to do it. Under his guidance, I've become a veritable whiz on a computer. In discussing my own process of empowerment with him, he laughed, "Yeah, Mom, we had a wimp rehabilitation program for you"—again, the power I gave my son came back to me. And over the years, I've raised my daughter, Kristen, to believe in herself and in her talents Now she is proving it to me, enriching this very book, and indeed my own career, with many forms of her expression. As a mom, I encouraged my kids to use their personal power. Now I know that they have the power to live healthy and effective lives.

When I was a child myself, however, I was told and thus believed that my purpose in life was to be a nice little girl. When I grew up, I found I was a very nice lady. By being "nice" I avoided situations that called for much power and yielded to others to avoid power struggles. I was acutely aware of my isolation and lack of support and had little sense of my own personal power.

Luckily, my children have taught me differently. Through the conflict-ridden process of being a mother and "just a housewife," I became aware of an awesome power and responsibility: to give life, to nurture, and to shape young beliefs and behaviors.

When I studied psychology in graduate school, I began to recognize a common thread through my courses and my own experience. Everyone needs to feel confident, to feel competent, to have a sense of power. I spent the next twelve years or so unraveling the fabric of my own beliefs and behaviors, and letting go of those that held me back. Bit by bit, I began to reweave the pieces. The new attitudes, skills, and habits have formed a cloak of power that is all my own.

Power comes from the Latin word *poder*, meaning "to be able." Everyone needs to be able, to be capable, to have a sense of personal power. At the heart of personal power is the knowledge that you are in charge of your life—that you have the ultimate responsibility for how you live it. In accepting more and more responsibility for your own self and your behavior, you gain personal power. In connecting and collaborating with others, you expand that power.

Power comes in many forms. We talk about buying power, staying power, power lunches, political power, power dressing, and a thing called clout. Certain roles—president, principal, policeman, parent—have power inherent in the job description. Success, in this country, is commonly measured by power in the form of money, status, or control and influence over others. With this kind of thinking, power is a pie and there are not enough slices to go around.

Power Associations

Power means different things to different people. Some positive associations are as follows:

- having choices
- making a difference
- being able to bring about change
- influencing others
- responsibility
- expressing one's uniqueness

Such associations make people desire power. (You can probably think of more.)

Sometimes the word makes people nervous because of its many negative associations.

- domination and oppression
- violence and abuse
- patriarchy and sexism
- rape and incest
- racism and slavery
- militarism and war
- manipulation, exploitation, and seduction
- dishonesty and secrets
- a burdensome responsibility for others

Power can be intoxicating and lead people to do inhumane things to others. Power can corrupt and destroy lives. Or it can create peace and understanding.

Power Games

Many kids these days play video games where they either explode something or get exploded; they learn that in order for one person to win, the other has to lose. The concept of "I want you to lose so that I can win" is deeply woven into the fabric of how we think and who we are. Unfortunately, this up/down, win/lose model of power is a way of life that has existed long before video games. This classic model for power struggles, punctuated by skirmishes for control, can edge immature people with poor impulse control into violence.

We cannot have healthy relationships if people are always on guard or attacking/counterattacking. We cannot have a win-win family if we constantly make others wrong so that we can be right. We cannot have healthy children if they get unhealthy messages and operate from a distorted value system that they consider to be "normal."

Basically there are two power games we can play.

- **Power Sharing.** Based on respect, caring, compassion, and support, people share power with each other. Cooperative, mutual, nurturing partnerships enhance and expand everyone's personal power. As people share power, the power increases.

or

- **Power Taking.** People who lack a sense of personal power often try to get it at another's expense. They dominate and disempower others. They may use any means, including violence, to gain control. In their "me versus you" thinking, they put others down so that they can feel one up. Always competing with others, they think they are okay if they are better than, or stronger than, or smarter than others. They try to feel good at someone else's expense, but it doesn't work. Self-esteem is not possible in this very common, win-lose power struggle. One person may appear to win, but the other is resentful. No one actually wins.

When we view power competitively, in up-down/win-lose terms, the idea of kids, wives, or husbands having power may be seen as a personal threat. Aware of only two options, parents (or siblings), not wanting to lose, will fight to keep others from winning.

When we move beyond the dominant/submissive definition of power, we discover that giving Johnny and Suzie a sense of their own power does not take it away from Mom and Dad. We build a family in which people are for, not against, each other. Just as all citizens have rights in a democratic society, a winning family honors the rights of every member.

In the divorce arena, power games can result in parents

fighting to win a custody battle with little regard for what is best for their children. Children are the victims in this win-lose system. A positive alternative to a legal battle is mediation, in which a skilled mediator helps both parties figure out what is best for them and for the children.

The Four Dimensions of Power

Imagine four people in a room together, each representing one stop on the spectrum of power. There's Mr. Powerless, who is helpless, dependant, insecure, and uninformed. There's Ms. Powerful, who is confident, capable, in control, and a risk taker. Mr. Empowering is supportive, encouraging, and challenging, while Ms. Overpowering is dominating, manipulative, arrogant, and pushy. Who would be attracted to each other? What would each one's spouse be like? Who would be drawn together? Who would avoid each other?

We have all been affected or hurt in some way by an overpowering person—a parent, teacher, friend, boss, or even a stranger. The object of this person's game is to gain power at another's expense. Some common tactics include

belittling, demoralizing and discouraging another • changing the rules
withholding support • intimidation • keeping secrets
blocking, weakening, or destroying connections.

"Divide and conquer" is an ancient strategy used around the world. In American society, we have been fragmented from our family and friends, from our ethnic roots, from our communities and neighborhoods, from Mother Earth. In our quest for individuality, competition, and progress, we have become separated from other ethnic groups, believing that their well-being directly threatens our own. Constantly on the move, many people feel alienated, disconnected, and lonely.

Reconnecting and Mending

If we have lost our power by being divided and conquered, we can regain it by reclaiming and mending our missing pieces. We can gain power by turning to others to share our common experience. As we connect with others around us, we can heal ourselves and at the same time increase our personal and collective power.

In a Mexican barrio, a laborer gathered together other women living in the same area. Although they lived very close to one another, they didn't know each other at all. As they sewed together, they discovered they had things in common. Each one was being battered. They realized that they were not alone, or crazy, or at fault.

They decided to do something to stop the abuse. Each woman got a whistle. They pledged that if any of them was abused, they or one of their kids would blow the whistle. The other women would immediately gather around her house in a circle banging on pots and pans. "That simple and empowering action began to transform the cycle of abuse in the barrio and change the relationships fostered among the women, within other relationships, and in how they saw themselves and their own power."[2] The single action of telling the truth led them out of isolation and into empowerment.

If we have been divided from ourselves—from our bodies, minds, emotions, spirituality—we can regain our power by reclaiming the missing pieces. When we accept our negative and abused parts and forgive ourselves, we become integrated and whole. As we love and embrace our wounded inner child, we can heal our lives. In honoring, supporting, and having compassion for ourselves and others, we can tap into our deepest power. From this source of strength we can draw the courage to meet life's challenges.

Violence: The Abuse of Power

Of all the industrialized nations, the United States is the most violent.[3] Women and children are the primary victims. Men are the primary perpetrators. Conditioned to accept violence and trained to commit violence, men have difficulty talking about how it has affected them—as targets of violence, as victims of child abuse, rape, or war.

Violence is the number-one health hazard in this country, more threatening than cancer, heart disease, or even automobiles. And it is addictive. Although domestic violence is a difficult issue to address, it must be discussed. Silence means acquiescence, tolerance, and acceptance.

- Next to illness, the primary cause of death in children under one year of age is homicide.[4]
- One out of three girls and one out of six boys face sexual abuse in some form before the age of eighteen.
- Americans spend two and one-half billion dollars per year on guns.
- The greatest single cause of injury in women is battering, and it happens to an estimated 4 million women per year.

Children raised in violent homes are victims. They learn violence as a way of life. They do unto others what was done unto them or what their parents did to each other, and the violence repeats. Studies show that boys raised in violent households become perpetrators, while their sisters learn to accept abuse by others.

Violence of all kinds is reaching epidemic proportions in American families. When children are abused, as adults their inner rage threatens us all. Abusive families therefore are public, not private, problems; they affect all levels of society.

Violence has become so widespread in our society that we

have come to accept it as normal. More violent deaths occur annually in New York City than have occurred in the last thirty years of war in Ireland! This is *not* normal. The leading cause of death of young black men is homicide. This is not normal.

The former chief of police of Minneapolis, Anthony V. Bouza, commented on these concerns at a National Conference on Violence: "For centuries women have been raised to accept their fate as victims and therefore to think and act like victims. If they were abused, they were led to believe that they somehow 'deserved' it. But those days have got to end for all women." According to Bouza, the police and the criminal justice system "must abandon their convenient myths of male authority and power"[5] and treat women differently. This does not just mean respect; it means the sharing of power. When women are put on a pedestal, they are set up to disappoint others and thus "deserve" punishment. In countries where women are valued and empowered, crime against women is not a problem. In winning families both husband and wife have dignity and they are of equal importance. The work and contributions of each are valued and appreciated.

If you live in an abusive home, be responsible for your own safety and that of your children. It is essential that you find someone to talk to. Get help. Visualize what you want for yourself, and find the courage to make appropriate choices. Think about timing. Protect yourself and your kids from harm. *This is your right.*

If you were raised in an abusive family, instead of repeating past mistakes, you can learn from them. Remember what it was like for you. Instead of wounding your children, you can heal yourself. You didn't deserve the abuse you received; neither do your kids. Seek information and treatment. Get support. Believe in yourself. Develop a vision of hope to move away from the destructive patterns of your past.

Gender and Power

The ideal, romantic view of the sexes in our culture defines masculine as dominating, superior, and controlling; in other words, to be masculine means to be overpowering. When boys act in these ways, parents may say "Boys will be boys" and let them escape the consequences. The romantic definition of feminine is passive, pleasing, sweet, obliging; in other words, to be feminine means to be powerless, and parents smile in approval at their nice little girls. These cultural definitions of power lock us into unhealthy win/lose power struggles. They teach us to create dysfunctional families.

At different times and in different cultures, children have grown up in less restrictive cultural molds. I was amazed to learn that the word virile comes from the same Latin root as the word virtue! To be an adult male had other healthier expectations then. And in ancient cultures, the word power meant *to serve*. Author Paula Gunn Allen discussed images of male power in her Native American tradition:[6]

> A man, if he's a mature adult, nurtures life. He does rituals that will help things grow, he helps raise the kids, and he protects the people. His entire life is toward balance and cooperativeness. The ideal of manhood is the same as the ideal of womanhood. You are autonomous, self-directing, and responsible for the spiritual, social and material life of all those with whom you live.

The women's movement in America has done much to challenge attitudes toward sex roles and to blur power roles along gender lines. Today more and more men are rethinking and challenging the restrictive cultural definitions of manhood. Realizing that the economic security of the family is not the only or even the most important domain, they are rediscovering their innate capacity to bond with and nurture their children. They are tapping freeze-dried parts of themselves and are making new choices. Men are also learning to be better friends and important resources for each other. And more and more couples are striving for partnership relationships where they share power rather than fight for it.

Family Empowerment

On a national level, parents are joining with others to make America more "family friendly." Parent Action is a newly formed national lobby dealing with the concerns and well-being of the 35 million families in the United States with children under eighteen. Connecting with others, parents can now begin to shape a unified voice and a vision of empowerment.[7]

Dr. T. Berry Brazelton, Parent Action co-chair, pediatrician, and author, states, "I want to empower young parents to get in there and get what they need. I want to fight for parent power. Our culture is in grave danger and it's because we're not paying enough attention to strengthening our families."[8]

The family unit is a basic building block in society. Traditionally, it has been a source of identity, strength, and stability for its individual members and the community at large. If a family is a battleground for personal power struggles, people are victimized. When, on the other hand, members of a family feel a sense of personal power, they don't have to fight for it. Husbands and wives can empower each other in an egalitarian relationship. They can empower their children and see to it that all can get their needs met and no one is victimized. Powerful families, in which members share power, can renew the entire society.

As parents we have tremendous power over our children's lives. We can empower children by offering them choices and by encouraging them to be strong and smart. We can also empower them by teaching them

- to be respectful—of themselves and others
- to be responsible for their behaviors
- that they have personal body rights
- to be assertive
- to be sensitive
- to be nonviolent
- to avoid dangers but to fight their battles

We can raise our sons to be sensitive and strong men who are not abusive. We can raise our daughters to be strong women who will not be battered. We teach these things best when we honor these qualities in our families and model them in our own relationships.

People with high self-esteem, who value themselves and others, do not tolerate abuse. They know they don't deserve it.

Our homes can be a refuge—a haven of love and safety, a source of strength and support. You have the power to create a supportive and peaceful family where people are for, not against, each other. Children need to feel safe at home. So do you.

13

For Your Own Good: Discipline Without Damage

> "Why do I so frequently need to be protected
> from those who love me?"[1]
>
> *Ashleigh Brilliant*

"Spare the rod and spoil the child." We all heard it when we were young. Most people understood it to mean that if you don't want a spoiled child—obnoxious, surly, and nasty—you've got to hit

them once in a while. The original meaning of this saying is quite the opposite, however. Biblical scholars tell us that shepherds in earlier times had two tools—a staff and a rod. Contrary to modern belief, the rod was not used for hitting; it was used gently—to guide the sheep in the desired direction.

Looking at the statement with new eyes, it rings even more true. Children need to be guided. If they are not guided—or are misguided—they will be "spoiled." If an adult overindulges a child without giving guidance, this will be detrimental to the child's character. But children cannot be spoiled by too much love! They are spoiled by a *lack* of love and guidance.

It is tragic that the original meaning of this quotation has been twisted to justify child abuse. By trying to *not* spoil children, parents have damaged them, instead.

The word discipline is also frequently misinterpreted. When I ask parents what comes to mind when they hear that word, they respond with "punishment," "force," and "hitting." Yet the word discipline has the same root as the word disciple, meaning pupil or learner. The purpose of discipline is to teach in such a way that children can learn, and to help children develop their inner guidance system so that they can function responsibly by themselves. They need to learn *self*-discipline with little things so they have the strength to deal with larger issues later on.

The short-term goal of discipline is to guide behavior on a daily basis and to protect children from hurting themselves and others. In the long run, discipline should help children become self-disciplined and take over the responsibility for their own behavior. They need to learn to rely on themselves, but this process takes time.

Behavior is an expression of how we feel about ourselves. Misbehavior is much less a problem in high self-esteem families. Building self-esteem in your children is your best insurance against behavior problems.

Natural and Logical Consequences

People who grow up in rural settings learn a lot about life from nature. If you plant and take care of your garden, there will be a harvest. If you don't milk the cow, she will dry up. Natural consequences are a natural occurrence. The connections are direct and clear.

In some settings, individuals in families, neighborhoods, and communities function as parts of interdependent systems and are accountable to each other. Extended families provide diverse role models, and there is a sense of connection even between unrelated adults and children. For individuals today, however, this lifestyle is the exception rather than the rule.

Today, children have fewer adults involved in their lives. They spend less time with parents and more time with the TV. Most television programs, however, do not teach natural consequences—the pain, burials, and rebuilding that happen *after* the story ends. Children miss learning about the cause-effect, action-reaction cycles of life. Removed from the lessons of natural consequences, we must rely on logical consequences to help children learn these skills.

Logical consequences[2] are structured situations based on mutual rights and mutual respect, that permit children to learn from the reality of the social order. These consequences must be related, respectful, and reasonable.

One day, for example, while doing errands with my young children, they started fighting in the back seat of the car. I was distracted and irritated and could have yelled, "You're going to lose your allowance," "You're grounded," or some other threat of punishment. Instead, I pulled the car off the road and turned off the engine. Very soon they stopped and asked, "What happened, Mom?" I softly explained that I couldn't drive with so much noise because it distracted me; I would have to wait until they quieted down. It worked like a charm—for about two miles. After a few repeats, they got the point.

It's important to have fair rules and attainable expectations. State them clearly so that everyone understands. It's also important that children see the connection between cause and effect—rowdiness, for example, causes Mom to pull the car off the road. When they know what is expected and don't comply with the rules, they learn from the consequences of that behavior.

Consequences must be related, respectful, and reasonable—and never put your kids in danger. Cause-effect thinking skills empower children to see relationships and make wise judgments. They will, for example, more easily understand that smoking causes cancer, that diet and lifestyle affect health, and that spending more than they have means financial trouble. They learn to think for themselves.

If children do not know what is expected of them, they may be confused by consequences. When children know what behavior is expected and don't comply with the rules, they learn from the consequences of their misbehavior. When they know what is expected and do comply with the rules, then they are rewarded with a sense of accomplishment, importance, and increased self-esteem.

Rescue Behavior

It is easy to interrupt the important process of learning from consequences. When we rescue others, they miss out on important lessons. The undesirable behavior is therefore likely to be repeated. For example:

	Case 1	**Case 2**
Action	Child turns off alarm.	Child spends money without anticipating future.
Result	Oversleeps, misses school bus.	Wants money for activity; has no money left.
Logical Consequence	Child must walk, bike, or take city bus; is late for school.	Child misses activity or has to earn extra money.
Rescuing Action	Parent drives child to school.	Parent gives child money.

The choice *not* to rescue takes a strong commitment to helping children learn about life from their own behaviors and from the social system. It must be appropriate both to the age and maturity level of the child and to the situation. It must also be done in an atmosphere of dignity and respect, love and firmness. The "art of parenting"—including wisdom and good judgment—is part of the picture.

For children with special needs, this can be particularly difficult. If they are to become self-sufficient, however, allowing them to learn from consequences can be a gift. A mentally challenged friend of mine described his childhood. "All my life my mom got me up, got me dressed, did everything. I never made a mistake. Then I moved into my group home and don't have anyone to take care of me anymore. Now I make a lot of mistakes, but that's okay because I'm learning how to take care of myself. And that feels good." Mistakes, or undesired results, are learning opportunities that give feedback about how to do it differently the next time. Don't rob children of those important opportunities.

There are times, however, when every parent chooses to practice rescue behavior. Sometimes situations occur that are damaging or difficult for a child to handle. A child who is being bullied or abused may not have the internal resources to deal with it. There are times when we need to rescue our children.

There may be times when grownups need to be rescued, too. Sometimes life deals us a hard blow; it's wonderful to know there are people we can call on when we're down and out. People get stronger by asking for help and support once in a while—until they get the strength to move on. The problem occurs when rescuing becomes a way of life, when someone always looks to others to take charge and solve problems, or when someone is always rescuing others. These behavior patterns disempower, weaken, and create low self-esteem and dependency.

Punishment and Rewards

"The floggings will continue until morale improves."

Anonymous

Many parents who use punishment believe their children *are* bad, and try to make them good by making them feel bad. This mostly doesn't work. When we feel bad, it's easier to do bad things. Most of us at one time or another have experienced the punishment system on some level, such as getting spanked for bad behavior. This system is based on external control, relying heavily on fear, anger, disappointment, and guilt. Some of the major disadvantages of the punishment system are as follows:

- Parents assume they are responsible for their children's behavior. When kids misbehave, parents feel guilty and ask, "Where did I go wrong?"
- Parents make all the rules and decisions and expect compliance (obedience), which often leads to resistance.
- Children are not allowed to make decisions or define their own standards of behavior.
- Parents use negative strategies to enforce their will— yelling, ridicule, criticism, blame, put-downs, labeling— all of which damage self-esteem.
- Behavior that is controlled by an authority figure usually lasts only while that person is present.

Many parents have said, "I'm going to teach you a lesson." More often than not, the "lessons" children learn from punishment are not at all what the parents had hoped to teach. A thirty-four-year-old woman told me that she vividly remembers the time her parents sent her down to the bottom stair in the basement to finish her dinner after she complained that she couldn't chew the meat left on her plate because it was too gristly. When I asked her what she learned from that, she said, "I learned that my parents didn't believe me, even if I was telling the truth. I learned that I was less important than their 'clean your plate' rules, and I hated them for humiliating me."

A parent's intention in punishment, to stop unacceptable behavior, is honorable, but the way they go about it leaves something to be desired. The true goal of punishment is to force submission ("I'll show you who's boss") or to get retaliation. Parents may stop the child's unwanted behavior, but damage the child and the relationship in the process. When children are deliberately hurt by parents whom they trust, love, and depend upon, they receive a powerful negative message.

Children learn about themselves by observing how they are treated, then drawing conclusions. Children who are mistreated may conclude that

- they are not okay; they are bad
- they don't deserve love; they deserve hate
- their parents don't love them, but hate them
- their parents are bad, cruel
- they deserve to be punished
- they cannot trust their parents or anyone else
- it is okay to hurt people
- the world is not a safe place

When these conclusions become their truth—when they believe that they deserve it—they may create punishing relationships (for themselves or others) throughout their lives. When they believe that they are bad, they feel shame and their sense of self-worth is shattered.

Think back to a time when you were punished as a child. What were your feelings toward your parent(s)? What did you learn? How did you feel about yourself?

When parents vow "to teach them a lesson," the children probably learn fear, distrust, hatred. When parents use force and violence, they teach children either to be violent themselves, or to be victims. When parents "make them behave," they raise children who are passive and fearful.

On the surface, rewarding children for their behavior may not seem to be as potentially damaging as punishment, but it can produce similar results. Children begin to feel manipulated. They look to and depend on others (external validation) for a sense of worth. They learn to "perform" to win their parents' attention and approval. They learn to become people pleasers, trusting others more than they trust themselves. After a time, they come to resent the rewards as much as the punishments.

Creative Family Management

Many parents repeat what *their* parents did, even though they hated it. Many use punishment, even though they swore they never would. Yet, there are many better ways to work with people. Here are some healthier options.

- **Suggest.** "It might be a good idea to ____."
- **Ask** for a favor or a change in behavior.
- **Offer an alternative** activity or location. "It's not okay to be so wild in the living room; go play in the yard."
- **Say no.** "No, you may not do that. It's dangerous." A serious look and a low voice will let them know you mean it.
- **Plan ahead.** Always keep a toy or book "up your sleeve" in case of an emergency, or a long wait.
- **Communicate clearly** what you want and how important it is to you. Eye contact and a gentle touch helps the message get across.
- **Remove the temptation.** Separate the kid from the problem.

- **Substitute.** If a child is heading for trouble, head him or her off with something more interesting. If a toddler has found something dangerous, take it away while presenting something that's more fun.
- **Team up with them.** Try the "ten minute pick-up" and make a game out of picking up toys. Race against the clock.
- **Appreciate** and cheer their efforts and their successes (See Appendix A).
- **Ignore small misbehaviors.** It may be wise to overlook some things, to do nothing—especially if you or your kid are having a bad day.
- **Keep them informed.** If a child knows what to look forward to, he or she can be more prepared for it. Talk about future events.
- **Focus** on what your children like to do that can happen after something they don't want to do. Try this formula: "When ____, then ____." "When you get your pajamas on, then we'll have time to cuddle and read a good story." Build in a reward.
- **Use nonverbal signals.** I got tired of reminding my young ones to buckle up their safety belts, so I tried something different. I'd tap them on the knee. They quickly got the message.
- **Distract them.** Divert their energy. On car rides when the kids were thirsty, I would tell them to lick their lips. It worked many times!
- **Make believe.** "Your teddy bear is lonesome for you and wants you to come to bed."
- **Outsmart them.** When walking with my little nephew, he complained of being tired. I suggested we run instead! It was fun and we got there faster.
- **Become a detective.** Figure out what's behind the undesirable behavior. Check, for example, their nutrition,

whether they have food allergies, or if they are tired or upset about something. Figure out what your children need. Help them find a better way to get their needs met than misbehaving.

- **Write notes.** I'd jot down chores for my kids to do after school. After establishing this as a form of communication, it became routine.
- **Take turns.** Say, "First we'll do what I want, then we'll do what you want." In this way, everyone wins.
- **Signal.** Advance notice is fair and makes good sense in driving and in parenting. Announcing that you have to leave in ten minutes allows kids to shift gears and complete what they're doing. Setting a timer can help to make them aware of limits.
- **Relax your standards.** Instead of expecting a perfectly made bed, for example, realize that some ideals are not worth daily battles. Pulling up the blankets was a compromise that worked for me. One way to deal with a messy bedroom is to close the door.
- **Break down** a large task into manageable pieces; encourage them. Celebrate their progress.
- **State your expectations very clearly.** Instead of saying, "Clean your room," say "Pick up the toys on the floor, make your bed, and put away your clothes." Then, "Tell me when you're done."
- **Let children know your limits.** When I announced "pajama time" and no one moved, I'd begin to count slowly to three. They knew I meant it, and would move by the time I got to "thr . . ."
- **Say nothing.** Sometimes it's best to bite your tongue, for example, when you're in a bad mood and know you would hurt them.
- **Use words that empower.** Instead of, "You can't go out until ____," say "You may go out when ____." Rather

than, "Because I said so," teach them; "Because when I did that, something bad happened." Moving from words of control to words of empowerment leads to cooperation rather than resistance.

- **Be playful.** Perhaps you have turned a toddler's spoon into an airplane full of food. I once overdramatized great disgust and nausea on finding dirty underwear in the bathroom and found it to be quite effective. When I'd notice untied shoelaces on a walk with my children, I'd try to step on them.

There are many ways to get what we want. The methods above avoid direct confrontation and punishment. You can get things done more easily if you avoid power struggles. And self-esteem will remain intact.

Motivation

With rewards, as with punishment, children learn to focus on trying to please those who have power over them, whether they want to or not: "I will do ___ so you will think I'm okay." When parents give stars for getting dressed, for example, and scoldings for being slow, kids feel manipulated.

A better approach is to peek in on their progress, saying "Hooray, you got your shoes on. Good for you, you're almost ready." Celebrate their progress, their growth. This reflects their small achievements back to them and helps them to intrinsically feel good about themselves. Tomorrow they may tell themselves (self-talk) the same thing: "Good for me, I'm almost ready."

With the reward system, tomorrow the child may again want a star or some other bribe to externally motivate him or her to get dressed. This outside focus leads to the development of external-locus-of-control people (see Chapter 21), who lack self-confidence and always look to others to tell them what to do.

Rewards, in moderation, are okay. Don't stop rewarding your kids. The ultimate goal, though, is for children *to want to* get dressed, practice piano, or keep their room clean, without involving time or energy on the parents' part. This attitude is more likely to result from the encouragement/support method.

Physical punishment doesn't change someone's mind. It may change behavior for a while, but it doesn't change opinions about the behavior itself, except perhaps to entrench it. Fear is a poor motivator.

When people are blamed and punished, they feel as if they have been attacked or violated. They may react by

- being defensive
- making excuses
- trying to protect themselves
- wanting to withdraw
- being afraid
- giving in (complying)
- becoming defiant
- becoming a perfectionist ("If I were perfect, I might be okay.")
- lying, cheating, or covering up

Once parents decide that they want children to be self-disciplined, they must discipline themselves to change old, punishing patterns of behavior and to model new behaviors. Once parents decide that they do not need to control—that they can trust children to learn from the consequences of their behavior—they can give up punishment and the associated feelings of distrust and resentment. They can move from an autocratic to a more democratic leadership style. With the natural/logical consequences approach,

- children are responsible for their own behavior.
- they are allowed to make their own decisions and to learn

from their successes and their mistakes.

- children learn from the reality of the natural and social order rather than from forced compliance to the wishes of authority figures.

This system of discipline focuses on the whole child—not only on their behavior. The goal is to teach the child *self*-discipline, *self*-direction, and *self*-responsibility. Since parents won't always be around to tell children what to do, they must instill *inner* discipline and help the children develop the ability to think, to judge, and to make decisions on their own. They must also model the behavior they want to see in their children. Example is the best teacher.

"It is easier to control than to teach," writes Dr. Stephen Glenn, an author and national consultant. "Teaching requires time, planning, and patience, but it lasts longer, gives clearer direction, and builds a foundation for a system of value. Dogs need to be controlled. Children need to be taught."[3]

Parents must realize that every child is frisky and mischievous at times. It is how they express their individuality and aliveness. If they want to do something and it doesn't hurt them, let them do it. Give them the freedom to be who they are. All normal kids act out once in a while; they are testing their environment. It's important to allow them self-expression while also setting limits.

When I had two little ones at home, I made up a name— "Boobledink"—to express mild displeasure. If, for example, someone would poke a finger in the icing of a birthday cake, I'd say, "You Boobledink," with partly serious displeasure. It helped make a point and kept me from using hurtful labels such as "bad," "brat," "stupid." Even now, I sometimes call my grown children that, and we laugh about it.

It's important to be aware of the degree of seriousness of the mischief. If it's serious, it should be dealt with, but there may be wisdom in letting little things slide. *Choose your battles carefully.*

It's also important to look for the cause of undesirable behavior and deal with that. Misbehavior is a signal that something isn't right. They may be tired, hungry, or reacting to something in their diet. Or they may need attention, be discouraged, or feel powerless. Get to the underlying feelings. *Help them to talk it out, so they don't have to act it out.*

You can create a winning family in which no one has to lose. You can have a winning team in which parents are positive, encouraging coaches who correct when it is necessary and give praise when it is deserved. Kids need attention, feedback, and the awareness that they are fulfilling your expectations. Parents who are coaches get positive results.

Coaches expect the best in their players and communicate that sentiment to their team. They believe in them and inspire them to greatness. The team members don't want to disappoint the coach, so they do their best.

Coaches are teachers who explain how to do things better. One dad, for example, observed his daughter using a hammer. Seeing her clumsiness, he stopped her, took the hammer, and showed her the correct way to use it. Giving it back to her, he asked her to try it that way. As she hammered more effectively, Dad encouraged her and celebrated her success.

Look for opportunities to share your knowledge and your skills. You know so much, and your children have so much to learn. Teaching them empowers them and sets up positive contact between you.

Finally, coaches spend time correcting undesirable and unacceptable behavior, and do so without discouraging or demoralizing the players. In *The One-Minute Manager*, Kenneth Blanchard and Spencer Johnson[4] outline this simple plan.

1. Let them know you want them to learn and grow and that you will correct them at times. Correcting them does

not mean you don't like them or that you're rejecting them, but that there's a better way.

2. Correct behavior while it's happening or as soon as you are aware of it. Deal with them in private.

3. Tell them that what they did was not acceptable. Describe the behavior, being specific, firm, and kind.

4. Tell them what you think and feel about that behavior, being clear but not angry.

5. Pause and let it soak in.

6. Touch them, smile, or say kind words to show that you have not rejected them, that you are on their side. Tell them that you value them but that the specific behavior is unacceptable.

7. Forgive and forget it. It's over.

We must deal with unacceptable behavior—in our kids, spouses, and friends, and in ourselves. How we do this makes a difference. If we do so in a caring, firm way—keeping our sense of humor—we will make a difference in the self-esteem of our children and ourselves.

> If I keep from commanding people, they behave themselves.
> If I keep from preaching at people, they improve themselves.
> If I keep from imposing on people, they become themselves.[5]
>
> *Lao Tzu*

14

Guidance in the Age of TV

"If this is the age of television,
I intend to find another age to live in."[1]

Garrison Keillor

On a trip to Nepal, I visited a village at the edge of a jungle inhabited by rhinos, tigers, and wild boars. In the river there were crocodiles. Children growing up in that environment are surrounded by imminent dangers—and learn very early how to avoid them. Everyone in the village knows that the rhinos leave their feeding ground after dark to go elsewhere to sleep. Young children must be taught—as I was taught—to stay off the path when the rhinos might be coming through. They must not only learn how to avoid dangerous animals but also, how to deal with them if they meet them. Nepalese children taught me what to do if I were to meet a rhino: climb a tree—fast!

Every culture has teachings that are transmitted from parent to child. American parents don't usually have to teach their kids how to deal with rhinos, but they do need to guide them in many other ways. Parents need to forewarn their children and protect them from the numerous hazards that prevail in urban, sub-urban, and rural environments. There are poisons under the kitchen sink and in the medicine cabinet, pollutants seeping into the water, and escaping into the air. There are toxic waste dumps that should be avoided. Likewise, there are mental poisons parents must be alert to, many of them running loose on the TV set.

In the past, a skull and crossbones warned against household dangers and poisons. Nowadays kids use that symbol to decorate their skateboards, notebooks, and clothing. Somehow we need to label the hazards that truly threaten ourselves and our children. Then, instead of indulging in worry, we can turn our concern into positive action.

TV and Culture

Since its invention, television has been an unprecedented force in our culture. It has expanded our perspective and made the world a smaller place. The impact of TV on the way we think, feel, and behave is as enormous as the invention of the printing press in the 1400s. Each of these technological advances has revolutionized human communication.

The typical American household has its TV on for an average of forty-five hours per week (that's six and a half hours a day!).[2] Does your household watch more or less? Think of the role TV plays in your family. Is it a hearth? Is it a family activity, or a family "passivity"? Is it a companion? Is it a lifeline? Is it a baby-sitter? Remember your relationship to TV in your childhood. Imagine what your parents' early years must have been like without it.

The hours spent viewing TV and videos and playing video games are hours not available for actively participating in the "real world," or playing, or being involved with friends and family.

Watching television is an individual activity that generally discour-ages interaction with others ("Shhh!"). As viewing time increases, family communication time decreases. As family communication decreases, people grow more distant from each other, and may even forget how to carry on a good conversation.

On the other hand, television (and all other media—movies, videotapes, computer games, and interactive video) has immense educational potential. Research shows that television viewing is a highly complex, cognitive activity, during which children are actively involved in learning.[3] Unfortunately, TV tends to address our lowest common denominators as a culture, and, for all its benefits, it can be a degrading influence on our society. If TV becomes a major influence in our lives, our personal self-worth can likewise be negatively affected.

Young children depend on their environment to learn about life, about how this world works, about how to think, feel, and behave. Like sponges, they soak in every piece of information, and believe that it is true. Yet, TV programming is mostly based on fantasy, and is not intended to be a teacher of values, appro-priate behavior, or skills. Impressionable and trusting, children assume that television gives an accurate view of the way things are. Younger children are particularly vulnerable to negative in-fluences, since, up to age seven, they have difficulty distinguishing between reality and fantasy. Information and misinformation alike become part of their reality, their belief system.

Our unconscious accepts everything as "truth," even that which is not true; it cannot distinguish between fact and nonfact (see Chapter 17). Since TV is such a powerful medium, children may be more likely to internalize the values it teaches than to believe what their parents teach them, or even what they know from their own experience. For children raised on a heavy TV diet, television replaces direct firsthand experience and can actu-ally become "reality" to them. A TV version of reality can lead

to confusion, pain, and real-life addictions when real-life problems come along.

Children want and need guidance. They look first to their
parents, who have traditionally been the primary teachers of
values, appropriate behavior, and life skills. Before the middle
of the twentieth century, children spent their waking hours interacting with parents, siblings, grandparents, and other extended
family members, or playing or reading alone or with friends.
Now they spend numerous hours each day watching television.
At the time of life when their minds are most impressionable and
most receptive, many children are being "parented" by television.
They learn to live by remote control.

As a project for an anthropology class in the 1970s, I joined
my children (then eight, eleven, and twelve years old) for Saturday
morning cartoons. Within three hours, we counted forty-two
commercials, mostly aimed at influencing children's food choices
and parents' buying habits. Together we rated the quality and
agreed that only two of the programs were amusing; the rest
were mediocre to poor, often using slapstick or violence as humor.
By the third hour, I was beginning to feel a bit nauseous (and a
little "crazy"), so I turned the TV off. My kids protested, saying,
"Mom, maybe the next one will be better."

In a complex society, television gives us art and information,
cultural touchstones, and ideally a public forum for ideas and
cultural exchanges. It's impact is far-reaching: More people can
see a terrible TV program in one evening than could see a Broad-
way show playing to a full house for twenty years. In some European countries, TV is broadcast only two hours a day. But American network and cable channels pack every single moment of
the day and night. Some shows contain excellent insights into
the human condition, messages about right and wrong, plots that
edify and stories that move us deeply. Most do not. Prime time
sitcoms, for example, are notoriously shallow attempts to keep
the audience tuned in between commercial breaks.

Advertising

Since money is the bottom line for stations and producers, television can be subliminally dangerous. Television advertising has become an institution in America, one on which our economy depends. Advertisers, in their competition for the consumer dollar, are becoming more and more skillful at manipulating the viewing public. A study done in Boston revealed that by the time a child reaches age eighteen, he or she has viewed 350,000 commercials.[4] Commercials confuse us and prey on our self-esteem, blurring the distinction between real and artificially manufactured "needs." Traveling to other countries points out the absurdity of our consumer mentality. We do not need VCRs; kids do not need designer clothes. Everything does not, ultimately, hinge on sex appeal. Our real needs are rather simple: food and shelter, safety, belonging, love, pleasure, respect, self-esteem. All other "needs" are really only wants, desires, and wishes—or things we've been talked into thinking we must have.

TV Values

When children look to television to learn about life, what do they learn? They learn to become consumers—never to be satisfied with what they have, always to "need" more things. They become frustrated and angry if they(we) cannot afford them. They learn to crave sugar. They learn to be self-critical perfectionists, or to seek immediate gratification of their desires and quick solutions to their problems—violently, perhaps—or they may learn to be passive and uninvolved with life. Granted there are exceptions to every rule, but our consumer culture depends on beliefs such as these.

- Happiness comes from material possessions and external conditions.

- Drugs will cure everything and are the only cure for physical problems.
- Violence is an acceptable and thrilling problem-solving behavior.
- Neuroses are normal. Body odor and calories are on everyone's mind.
- Women are preoccupied with invisible enemies like dirt, calories, and smells.
- Skinny is beautiful, and any other shape is abnormal or undesirable.

These ideas are all setups for low self-esteem. They instill notions that are destructive to our state of mental health. Yet these images are accepted in good faith by children hungry to understand life and how they should interact with their world.

A task force of the American Academy of Pediatrics concluded in 1985, after a sixteen-month study that

- Watching TV promotes obesity.
- TV encourages the use of drugs, alcohol, and tobacco by glamorizing them.
- TV's unrealistic sexual relationships may contribute to the risk of teen pregnancy.
- Repeated exposure to TV violence can make children both violent and accepting of real-life violence.[5]

Watch prime time TV some night and pay attention to the underlying messages about sex, alcohol, and violence. Notice statements about and attacks on self-esteem. Watch beer commercials during football season. With a world full of possibilities, these things are obsessions of American media culture. Is this what you want your children to learn—and to become?

A report by the University of Pennsylvania's School of Communication (1986) recently stated that the "family hour" on TV (which has the most children viewers) is, in fact, the "violence hour." The programs viewed in one week on the three major networks included 168 acts of violence, the highest rate of violence in the nineteen years since the study was first conducted in 1967.[6]

There is no question that violence in the media and violence and crime in society are related. According to the National Association for the Education of Young Children, "research demonstrates that watching violent programs is related to less imaginative play and more imitative play in which the child simply mimics the aggressive acts observed on television." Interactions involving toys based on characters of children's shows undermine children's creativity and imaginative play, which is essential to their development.[7] Teachers and day-care providers reported to me that after watching the Gulf War in their living rooms, children were much more aggressive in their behavior.

Most network-TV producers and programmers show no responsibility for the guidance and well-being of children. Their primary commitment is to the advertisers who fund their stations. They show programs to draw large audiences of consumers and do not concern themselves with the immense impact their programs or advertisements have on children. Thus it falls to parents, and others who care for and work with children—to vigilantly protect their innocence and well-being.

The past few years have brought some positive changes. There are more anti-drug messages, both on shows and in advertisements. The years of work on the part of Mothers Against Drunk Drivers (MADD) and other groups are paying off—alcohol advertisers now comply with stricter guidelines, and are starting to encourage responsible drinking.

TV in the Family

I remember life before television. We kids had lots of time to play—times that were perhaps the happiest of my childhood.

We would rollerskate, ride bikes, play games, and go on snake hunts. We learned to entertain ourselves. Since the introduction of television, this pattern has changed.

Without television, children and adults gain firsthand, hands-on experience of the world. They spend more time using their imaginations, interacting with people and participating in life. They have a more solid understanding of themselves as individuals and a genuine connection with the world they live in. They are more aware of their place in the community. They are more creative at play and work. They have a foundation for building real human relationships, and are less afraid to speak up and let their own voices be heard. They take life at its own pace. With television, children may be exposed to too much beyond their comprehension or developmental stage.

It is a parent's responsibility to monitor the quality of the media their children watch. Watch the shows they like. Talk with and listen to your kids. See what messages they're getting from the shows they watch. Limit viewing time. Select in advance the best programs to watch. Involve children in decision making. There are many fine programs on science, art, culture, entertainment, music, and sports. Public television is a good place to start. Some network shows are better than others. Properly regulated, TV can enhance your family's life—as can many other activities. Watch it together at times. It can be a nice ritual. It used to be a special treat for the kids to stay up late and watch "Star Trek" with their dad. It was a special time for cuddling and talking about what they saw, what they thought about the world.

If you are not able to monitor your child's TV watching 100 per cent of the time, make sure you teach him or her judgment skills. Ask your children questions about the programs they watch. Encourage them to understand what they are watching. Discourage them from passively staring at the screen. Ask them their opinions on the content of shows and commercials. "Do the girls you know really like toys like that?" "What's the dumbest commercial for a breakfast cereal you've ever seen?" "Did you learn anything from the TV today?" "Why do you think kids need so many toys?" "What's so funny about this cartoon? Can you explain it?" "Which shows that you watch make you feel smart?" The ability to know one's opinions and trust one's judgements is a key part of high self-esteem.

Television programs can be a springboard for telling your stories and discussing values. Talk back to the TV. Call your TV stations and let them know how you feel about the programs. Protest the violence and praise the fine shows. Use your consumer influence to communicate with advertisers and sponsors of violent programs. You might even involve your children in writing to broadcasters and companies that use violent images to sell toys and other products. Doing these things will empower them not to be victims of violence.

Children need your guidance to help them handle their physical, emotional, spiritual, social, and sexual development. They need your guidance to understand themselves and the world they live in.

- to learn to say no
- to be responsible
- to take good care of themselves
- to be careful of what they put in their bodies
- to be smart
- to use their talents and imagination
- to avoid trouble
- to solve problems

Make sure their TV viewing enhances these qualities.

It takes courage for parents to talk about some of these things. Yet, if kids can't talk with their own parents, who will they talk to? What will they learn? Who will they learn from?

There are many things in our modern world that are as

dangerous to youngsters as rhinos. Our awareness, guidance, support, and empowerment are the best gifts we can give our children so that they can learn to think for themselves and thus protect themselves. Ultimately, self-esteem is the best protection against the poisons and pitfalls that crowd our world.

15

Problem Solving

"To the questions of your life, you are the only answer.
To the problems of your life, you are the only solution."[1]

Jo Coudert

When I was a child and my brothers teased me, I ran to my mother, wanting protection for me and punishment for them. When I had a misunderstanding with my friends, I would not play with them again—or at least not until we forgot about it. I ran away from and avoided problems because I never learned how to face conflicts and get through them. I was unprepared for the challenges of the world and was afraid of them.

As a mother, however, I didn't want my kids to pull me into the middle of every argument they had. I wanted to empower them to solve their own problems. A friend with many adopted children once told me her secret formula: Whenever two children had a problem, she had them sit on a certain stair—"the stair of love and peace"—until they worked it through; then they could go play. Those children learned to resolve problems by themselves.

I tried this on my own children. Although they hated that stair, they soon learned that they were responsible for solving their problems. In effect, I stepped aside and allowed them to develop important skills. In learning to solve their little problems, they began to gain the skills, experience, and confidence to get through tougher situations.

Problems and conflicts are natural events in life. Everyone has them. We don't choose hassles, but we can choose how to react and how to deal with them. Some strategies intensify the problem and cause distance, distress, and low self-esteem. Other strategies de-escalate the conflict and bring about resolution, closeness, and joy. Without skills and confidence, every problem is a crisis. With skills and confidence, a problem is a challenge to take on, an event to deal with and get beyond.

It is not your job to fix other people's problems; that's everyone's own responsibility; but you can give support. If we solve problems for other people, we deprive them of the opportunity to gain competence, confidence, and personal power. In addition, our solutions may not be the best ones for them. Encourage children to solve problems in their own way.

Ask: Whose problem is this? That person is responsible for the solution. We can listen as they talk through their troubles. This often begins to alleviate a problem. It lets them know we care, lets them hear themselves, and helps them gain perspective. Then, ask what they can do to resolve their issue.

Children need to learn to take care of their own problems— and to overcome them. They need to learn to deal with disappointments, losses, and pain so that they know they can survive them. It can be difficult for us as parents to watch them struggle; we want to take away the pain. Yet children who have been overprotected will be incapacitated and overwhelmed by the first big problem they have to handle on their own. Kids who don't know how to deal with failure, disappointment, or loss are at risk.

We need to encourage and support children through their struggles—and believe in them. ("I've seen you solve some tough problems; I know you can get through this one, too.") We need to allow them to experience their own mistakes and failures and help them discover the joy of overcoming. Problems themselves don't necessarily overwhelm children, but self-doubt and lack of experience and skills do.

We need to share our own struggles with our children. If we pretend to have it together all the time, they may conclude that something is wrong with them for having problems. When we share our mistakes, our losses, our failures, and how we deal with them, they understand that we, too, experience disappointments—that we, too, are human. And they learn new ways of coping.

The more positive attention you give, the more you fill their basic human needs for safety, love, belonging, attention, and self-esteem, the fewer the problems you will have. If you ignore their needs, problems and misbehavior often result. There are always reasons—thoughts and feelings—underneath problems and misbehavior. They are but signals that indicate that something is wrong. *Behavior is an expression of how children feel about themselves.* To help resolve the problem, and thus the behavior, we must play detective and figure out what's really going on from the child's point of view.

Have family meetings to listen to each other and keep communication channels open. In dealing with family problems, first of all, believe that there is a solution; all you have to do is find it. Second, listen to each other to understand the situation clearly, and third, have the willingness and courage to make necessary changes. When all involved parties assume responsibility for the problem and the resolution, there's hope for a positive outcome.

One adolescent exhibited problem behavior as a result of the stresses of her blended family situation and. She wrote:

> My "family" became a constant clash of rage, caused and aggravated by lying, mistrust, and hurtful accusations. I was driven

out by hatred based on something I don't understand. In my self-destructive family it became clear that steps had to be taken to alleviate or avoid further stress. We created commotions, such as fussing, threatening, and running away (behaviors we had never before considered), desperate for a listening ear. We pleaded for a solution, but ended up escaping from problems that were beyond our control.[2]

Her acting out was merely a symptom of the real problems her parents refused to discuss or deal with. Running away from home was her best solution to a harmful situation she could not change, which might otherwise have ended tragically.

Barriers to Problem Solving

One reason that people are afraid of problems is that they don't know how to solve them. They may be using one of the following strategies:

- **Denial.** Although putting problems aside for a little while may help us to cope, we can't get through our problems if our heads are in the sand. And if our heads get stuck there, we're in real trouble!
- **Drugs.** This strategy alters the inner reality—the perception of the problem. With alcohol and other drugs, people can pretend that they have solved a problem because they can no longer feel it. Unfortunately, they are creating a more serious problem of addiction.
- **Distraction.** This strategy of avoidance can be a short- or long-term escape from the problem. ("Let's watch TV.")
- **Gunny-sacking.** Storing up the problems, anger, and pain solves nothing. When it builds up, a harmful explosion may result.
- **Blaming.** When we point our finger at others and resort to fault finding, we deny our own responsibility and our ability to change things. The persons who are blamed feel attacked and want either to counterattack or defend themselves.
- **Rejection.** Cutting people off may seem to solve a problem, but an important relationship can be damaged or lost. ("I never want to see you again.") Sometimes you may need time away from people you love; that's okay. But rejecting a person or a relationship can make life painful and lonely.
- **Fighting/Withdrawing.** One is aggressive; the other is passive. In our culture boys are often taught to slug it out, while girls learn to seek help or wait to be rescued. ("Put up your dukes!" versus, "Mommy! Help me!") Each of these behaviors, used alone, is a trap. It sets up couples for battering.
- **Personal attacks.** Name calling and "you" statements hurt the other, escalate the conflict, and often harm the

relationship. ("You are totally worthless.") Often we regret it later.

- **Rationalizing.** This strategy intellectualizes the pain to avoid feeling it. ("We're better off than the Joneses.") This only perpetuates the problem.
- **Defeatism.** If you believe there is nothing you can do to solve the problem, you will be powerless to do anything. ("It's hopeless.") You will remain helpless.

These strategies are useful for living with—not dealing with—problems. They are very common and they get us stuck. We may go through any of these states at one time or another, but they don't work ultimately because they avoid confronting our problems. Avoidance is a cop-out. To cope with and resolve problems, we must attend to them.

Many of these strategies go along with the win-lose approach. The goal is to "win" by proving that I am right and you are wrong. No one likes to lose; no one likes to be made wrong. An emotionally charged power struggle ensues from a win-lose solution and often escalates. Everyone's self-esteem is at stake: "If I don't win, I'm not okay; therefore I must win." The problem may appear to be settled, but it isn't, because the loser is angry and resentful. No one comes out winning.

A divorce, for example, can be a frightening power struggle. Both parents may fight to win a custody battle, even though neither wants the primary responsibility for raising the children. The kids get victimized in this wrenching process. Nobody wins. Everybody suffers.

When facing a problem, it helps to examine the underlying goal. Do you want to "win" at the other's expense? Or do you want to resolve the problem to everyone's satisfaction?

It is possible to solve problems with no one losing. Win-win solutions take time, energy, and self-discipline. Sometimes we have to bite our tongues so they don't get us into trouble. Win-win problem solving calls for direct, honest, and assertive communication, and the willingness to really listen and understand each other. It takes time, energy, and self-discipline. This approach is not easy, but it's worth it. Increased respect, intimacy, and enhanced self-esteem are the payoffs.

The goal of win-win strategies is to resolve a conflict so that both parties are satisfied. The focus is not on the persons, but on the solution—"What will we do about it?" The underlying attitude is respect—for oneself and for the other. Both must accept responsibility for the problem and be committed to resolving it without damaging the relationship.

Stepping Stones to Problem Solving

- **Believe** that your problem is solvable. Be positive, hopeful, and expect good things to come of it.
- **Determine ownership.** Whose problem is it? Everyone is responsible for solving his or her own problems. Don't solve kids' problems for them—unless they are in danger or in a situation that is overwhelming them.
- **Dissect the problem.** Running on a trail, my 4-year-old nephew fell down. He howled at the top of his voice. I asked where he hurt. "All over!" he cried. Then I asked if his chin hurt. "No." His knees? "No." His stomach? "No." We narrowed the pain down to sore hands. Then I knew where to bestow the healing kisses.
- **Don't try to figure out** who's right and who's wrong. Judgements get in the way of understanding. If a judgment is made too early, someone will not feel listened to, and the conflict will continue.
- **Evaluate the importance of the problem.** Tell how important it is. "This isn't very important, but I'd like to talk about it," or "This is very important to me!"
- **Speak in terms of "I want," or, "I feel,"** rather than

"You did this" or "You didn't do that." The I-statement model often resolves problem situations.

- **Use active listening skills.** Try to understand another point of view, another way of seeing a situation.
- **Express your beliefs, values, and opinions as your point of view,** not as The Truth.
- **Read between the lines.** Try to figure out what's going on underneath the words—fear? anger? a power struggle? protection?—and address that.
- **Listen to feelings.** Receptivity to how someone feels often unlocks a situation, and the solution becomes more apparent.
- **Be sensitive to timing.** Use good judgment about when to talk; (when people have time and are relaxed). If you are unsure, ask, "Is this a good time to talk?" Allow enough time for discussion. Also, discuss important matters after a meal; families have seven times as many fights before dinner than after.
- **Respond** to the other person; don't react. A response comes from a centered place. The difference between reaction and response, they say, is about ten seconds.
- **Ask for what you want.** "I just want you to listen while I tell you what I feel."
- **Be willing to make changes.** It's hard to accept, but negotiation can only happen if *both* parties are willing to give something up in order to reach a mutually satisfying result. Conflicts are resolved more quickly if priorities are understood.
- **Always learn from mistakes** and figure out how to do it better the next time.
- **Take time out if things get tense.** Take a break to cool down. Do something physical to release the tension. Set a time to talk again later.

- **Check out all assumptions.** "Do you mean ____?" "Are you saying ____?"
- **Look for the lesson behind the problem.** Figure out how you can avoid it in the future by learning from it.
- **Keep focused in the here and now;** pulling up ancient history muddles things.
- **Forgive others their mistakes** and ask forgiveness for your own.
- **Keep a sense of humor**—especially by laughing at yourself.
- **Rule out violence.** "Use your words," said a nursery school teacher, "not your feet, teeth, or spit." Violence does not solve conflicts, and it always has negative consequences.
- **Get help**—family mediation or counseling—if you are having trouble resolving problems. Do it soon, before problems get out of hand.

Problem-Solving Steps

"You may not be responsible for being down,
but you are responsible for getting up."[3]

Jesse Jackson

For many people, problems are stumbling blocks that present unwanted challenges, anxiety, and stress. With a shift in attitude and new skills, however, they can become stepping stones to deeper understanding and better relationships. This process of problem solving can be used in any situation, whether inter- or intrapersonal.

1. **Identify and define the problem or conflict.** What is really the problem? What exactly is wrong? Identify the

problem without blaming. Be aware of everyone's feelings and needs.

2. **Brainstorm for possible solutions.** Express and record all ideas as fast as you think of them. Sometimes the craziest, wildest ideas become the best with a little fixing up. No judgment or discussion should be allowed while brainstorming.

3. **Evaluate the alternatives.** Look at the consequences of each choice. Would it solve the problem or make it worse? Work together to find a solution acceptable to all parties. Give and take is necessary for a win-win solution.

4. **Choose the best solution.** All parties in the conflict need to find and agree to this solution. They must be committed to doing it.

5. **Implement the solution.** What changes need to be made? Who will do what? When will they do it? For how long? In some situations it may help to informally write out an agreement and sign it to avoid confusion. Decide when to evaluate how it's working.

6. **Follow-up evaluation.** Assess the results. Is the situation better, worse, or the same? If it is better, do you want to extend the contract? If worse, consider another solution from the brainstorming session and implement it. Be persistent until the problem is resolved.

When we know that we can get through conflicts without losing, we have no need to avoid or withdraw from them. When we acquire skills and experience in resolving touchy situations, our confidence grows, as does our self-esteem. And the more we learn, the more we have to teach our children.

"Every problem comes with a gift."[4]

Richard Bach

16

Touch

"Emotional CPR: one hug, one deep breath. Repeat."[1]

The recommended daily requirement for hugs is: four per day for survival, eight per day for maintenance, and twelve per day for growth.[2] Touch is vital to life. We need to be caressed, cuddled, and stroked as much as we need food. Babies who are deprived of touch can actually die; lacking stimulation and nurturance, their spines shrivel up.

A scientist from the National Institute of Health claims that a lack of touch and pleasure during the formative years of life is the principal cause of human violence. He observed that individuals and societies that experience and promote physical pleasure are also peaceful societies. The two exist in one's life in inverse proportion: "As either violence or pleasure goes up, the other goes down."[3]

Many children suffer touch disorders from their parents: from neglect (insufficient touch), from battering (painful touch of the wrong intensity), and from incest (inappropriate and violating touch).

For persons who have been abused, it makes sense that the

necessary healing should come through the same modality. If, for example, the abuse was verbal, then positive, loving words can be very healing. If the abuse was physical, healing can be facilitated through respectful, appropriate, loving touch. Touch can be a cruel and damaging violation of another person, or it can be a nourishing gift of love and pleasure for those we care for. The choice is ours.

We learned about touch from our parents. If they cuddled and hugged us a lot, we learned to enjoy touch. If they didn't touch us at all, we learned either to crave physical contact or to physically close ourselves off to others. If they punished and abused us—touching us violently—we probably learned to fear and avoid touch, or to punish and abuse others.

Premature or handicapped infants can experience neglect in touch due to being in an incubator or because of physical deformities. Studies show that parents of deformed children or of children with special needs use less touch initially. Physical therapists often need to work with these children to combat their "tactile defensiveness," or resistance to touch.

From the media, we learn to equate touch with sex, although sexual touch is only one of many types of physical expression. The kind of touch we need most is warm, affectionate, casual, and nonsexual. When we understand this, we can unravel the confusion and separate the two in our minds. Touch as an affectionate gesture is an art worth relearning.

In New Zealand some nurses work with a group of parents who are at risk of abusing their children—because abusive touch was the only touch they learned. Every week these parents attend a lecture on child rearing, have a cup of tea, and do the following exercises to practice the art of touch in a new, healthy, loving way.[4] It's important to establish that the body receiving this attention is in charge, and should give feedback. ("More!" "Harder." "Softer." "Stop that." Remember, the purpose is to inflict pleasure, not pain.) Treat your own children and spouse to this adapted New Zealand "weather report."

- **Snowflakes.** Tap fingertips rapidly on the other person's head, shoulders, and back, lightly, like falling snow.
- **Raindrops.** Tap fingertips simultaneously and with greater intensity.
- **Thunderclaps.** With cupped palms, clap hands across the person's back and shoulders. This makes a good noise; be careful not to slap.

- **Eye of the tornado.** Circle thumbs across the person's shoulders and down either side of the spine using your fingertips to anchor the motion.
- **Tidal wave.** Slide hands in long strokes up and down the person's arms and across the back. Sound effects can be fun here.
- **Calm after the storm.** Rest hands on the other person's shoulders and breathe deeply. Slowly remove hands to about half an inch above the skin for a few moments. Step back slowly—it may feel to the other person as if your hands are still there! [5]

The nurses found a similar exercise to be a great success. One mother reported that she stifled an urge to hit her baby, and massaged his back instead—with far superior results! It's an enjoyable, relaxing, and self-esteem-enhancing gift—both to give and to get.

One mother told me that her child had difficulty getting to

sleep. She tried this massage and "he turned into Jell-o and was out." Another mom has turned this into a geography lesson as well. Before bed, she gives her twin sons what they call the "U.S. weather report," with snowstorms in the northeast, earthquakes in California, and so on, until the stormfront stops and the sun comes out. "My ten-year-old boys love it and do it to each other ... and to me! It's a bedtime ritual that makes my kids *want* to go to bed."

In an unusual school program, a professional acupressurist worked on twenty-three special education students with remarkable results: There were significant gains in cognitive, motor, social/emotional, and health areas. In other classrooms students have been taught how to push pressure points that block energy and hold tension in the body. When they say "Push my buttons" to a classmate, they get a little massage. Parents and teachers alike have reported immediate improvement in behavior and self-esteem.[6]

Touch can be very therapeutic. Barbara told me about clashes with her nine-year-old daughter who entered "the age of contradiction." In order to mend the rift and tension between them, she made a concerted effort to do more touching. Over the next several months, she would pat her daughter on the shoulders and back, hug her more often, and hold her hand on walks. "As I increased the amount of physical contact, her acting out and resentment decreased. Eventually, the turbulent nines disappeared and she blossomed into a fun and happy ten-year-old child."

Child Abuse

"Those who cannot remember the past
are condemned to repeat it."[7]

Inscription at Dachau Concentration Camp Museum

Abuse—sexual, physical, emotional, and verbal, create enormous problems and pain for individuals, families, and all of society. It damages self-esteem and mental health, and destroys trust. We don't want to hear about abuse. We don't want to—or are afraid to—talk about it. But to break the cycle of violence, it must be discussed.

Sexual child abuse refers to any inappropriate sexual exposure or touch between an adult and a child. It is inappropriate when a child does not understand the nature of the request, or when a child is coerced through threats or deceit—such as, when an abusive father tells his daughter that this is "normal" affection. It is inappropriate when an adult takes advantage of a child's innocence, needs, or fears. Inappropriate touch by a parent is highly damaging to the child and to the parent-child relationship.[8] There are many reasons that incest has always been taboo in cultures around the world.

Overly severe physical punishment—hitting (with hands, fists, or objects), pinching, burning (with cigarettes, etc.)—is literally torture. It has caused unspeakable harm to individuals and widespread social violence. Corporal punishment and neglect can lead to psychopathology in children and misery in families. It is not right for people who say they love a child to hurt her or him in the name of discipline.

Authorities estimate that in the United States up to 90 percent of murders, rapes, and other violent crimes are committed by people who were child abuse victims themselves. Lee Harvey Oswald, Charles Manson, and Adolf Hitler—to name but three—were all victims of physical and emotional child abuse.

Behavioral patterns are handed down from one generation to the next. Children who are loved grow up to nurture others. Children who are rejected tend to become rejecting parents. Abused children become abusive parents. The patterns tend to repeat—generation after generation—unless we take the initiative to stop them.

Many of us who were abused as children deny it. Our parents were very important to us; we depended on them for survival. We needed to believe they were good and, therefore, we denied the abuse or made up excuses for their behavior—"I deserved what I got." "It was my fault." "I had it coming." We concluded that *we were bad* or else they wouldn't have treated us that way. Childhood abuse and neglect leaves us with an inner emptiness that we may try to fill by means of food, alcohol, drugs, sex, work, or money. These things don't fill in the hole—but they frequently become addictions.

Many of us don't want to remember the abuse because it was so bad; we may have needed to forget what was done to us. Many of us minimize the abuse: "It wasn't all that bad." "I was never hospitalized." "It could have been worse." Many of us hold in the old anger, afraid that we might explode and hurt someone we love or hurt ourselves.

If we deny the mistreatment, we probably don't recognize that our primary role models were negative. We don't realize, therefore, that we are automatically following those same negative patterns and inflicting similar abuse on our own children. Continuing the habits and repeating old mistakes, however, we become negative models for our own children, and, tragically, the pattern repeats for yet another generation.

As people begin to recognize their patterns, however, they can gain the freedom to choose differently. With awareness comes choice. We can unlearn damaging behaviors and relearn life-enhancing ones. Once we have the courage to remember the past and how our parents harmed us, we can make conscious choices about the future. With determination and support from others (perhaps professional therapy), negative situations can be turned around.

Says Dr. Brandt F. Steele, Chief psychiatrist at the Kempe Center for the Prevention and Treatment of Child Abuse,"

From early infancy, children of abusing parents are expected to be submissive, respectful, thoughtful and considerate of their parents. It is axiomatic to the child beater that infants and children exist primarily to satisfy parental needs, that children's needs are unimportant and should be disregarded, and that children who do not fulfill these requirements deserve punishment.

When abuse occurs in families, parents usually have some of the following traits:

A history of battering. Parents have learned that beating is the "right way" to discipline children. Quick to anger, they may have poor impulse control. Perhaps they learned those behaviors from their own parents, who may also have been abused. A pattern of emotional or verbal "battering" may also be prevalent.

A distorted view of the child. Parents may believe that a child is basically bad and deserving of punishment. They may also believe that about themselves. It's easy to *be* bad when you believe you're a bad person. Parents may justify abusive treatment, claiming it is necessary to prevent evil behavior from developing. A better way to get kids to be good is to believe that they *are* good—and help them believe that about themselves.

Unrealistic expectations. Parents may have expectations of the child—and perhaps of themselves—that are too high or impossible. They don't realize that children are immature. They may expect behavior that is developmentally impossible. A six-month-old, for example, cannot be potty trained. Young children are not always respectful and considerate of their parents. Nor can kids be expected to understand things like adults or behave like adults. Not understanding this, parents may inflict severe punishment for minimal infractions.

Parents may expect a child to fill their own needs. A mother, for example, who wants her daughter to love her as her own mother didn't, is asking for the wrong thing. Kids do not exist to satisfy their parents' needs. Parents, however, do exist to satisfy their children's. It is important to remember who is the grown up and that children need love and guidance. Parents who were not loved as children must also care for their own wounded inner child. In becoming aware of their own unmet needs, they can begin to heal them; then they won't (unconsciously) expect others to parent them.

Lack of warmth. Parents may not actually like their children. They may be unaware, unable, or unwilling to relate to and meet their children's emotional needs. For example, Mom may have felt unloved, and married for love but found loneliness instead. She—and her child—may give up hope of acceptance and love. Yet, hope is a spark. If you practice acceptance and caring, love will kindle on its own.

A negative focus. A parent seldom notices or mentions any good qualities in a child but rather is always catching him or her being "bad." The parent may withhold a privilege and love, or isolate the child to teach a lesson. Regardless of the child's efforts to please, the parent will find something to criticize, and the child rarely receives praise. Yet kids need appreciation and encouragement, just as parents do. Try flipping the focus and finding one likable or endearing quality about a child—a cute smile, perhaps—and then another, and another. The quality of the interaction will automatically improve.

Poor communication skills. Parents don't know how to really listen to their children. They forget to put themselves in their children's shoes and to see things from their point of view.

Seeing from another's perspective is an important skill—a skill that can be learned. Learning to really listen and to feel empathy and compassion can begin to transform a negative relationship (see Chapter 5).

Overuse or abuse of power. Perpetrators of violence often have a deep sense of powerlessness. Instead of enhancing their own personal power, they overpower others. Such parents believe that children must be taught "who is the boss" and should not be allowed to get away with anything. They are righteous about discipline and punishment. They may imagine that children are trying to anger or hurt them, often taking things personally and retaliating violently. ("I'll show you to talk back to me!") Adults who lack self-discipline are dangerous disciplinarians.

Overpunishment. Parents may not be aware of the limits beyond which punishment becomes abuse. For example, to sit a young child in a corner for five minutes may not be damaging. To do it for an hour is abuse. Children have a different sense of time. (For better ways to discipline, see Chapter 13.)

Isolation. The battering family has few close friends, family supports, or social activities. Family members feel alienated and do not know where to turn for help. One way to begin is with a phone call. Suggest a cup of tea or a walk to the park with someone. Visit a Parents Anonymous meeting in your area. No one needs to be alone!

Each year thousands of children are paralyzed, physically deformed, mentally damaged, and killed through abuse. There is a direct cause-effect relationship. When abuse occurs, damage results. Many parents don't realize how fragile a child's body is. Shaking a child can seriously hurt a her or him, causing mental retardation, permanent brain damage, and death. Striking a child's body is dangerous. One "good" slap on the cheek of a small child can bruise the brain and cause permanent retardation. Adults must learn to control damaging impulses. Parents who are afraid of hurting a child have reached a turning point. The next step is to: Take time out to cool off. Get away from the dangerous situation. Ask for help. Call the national toll-free number for ChildHelp, a crisis/referral line: 800-422-4453. Child abuse is 100-percent preventable.

What can you do if you witness a parent abusing a child? Try one of these statements.

"I know you want to do the right thing, but this is not good for your child."

"I know this is a tough time (age) for you, but this is not good for your child."

"Perhaps you were raised this way, but this is not good for your child."

"I know it's hard to be a good parent sometimes, but _____."

"You are the most important person in your child's life, and _____."

"I'm a mom/dad, too. Is there anything I can do to help?"

You might then offer a suggestion and support for that person and the child.

People don't generally wake up in the morning saying, "I think I'll whomp my kid today." As the day goes on and stress builds, something or someone "pushes a button" that "triggers" a reaction. It is important to learn about your buttons and triggers—and how to defuse them. What happened just before you "lost it"? Magnify that moment; unravel it. *You can choose to react differently.* What can you do to prevent it from happening again? If you need help in doing this, get it.

One dad decided he wasn't ever going to hit his kid again. He established a house rule for himself: *Hug instead of hit.* When this man was tempted to smack his kid, he would continue the movement with his arm, and instead of hitting, would surround the child in a big embrace. He would explain that the act was unacceptable but the child is very, very much loved! Another mom told me that, even though she had decided to not spank her daughter when stressed out, she found herself acting "on automatic." "I slapped her on her bare bottom once and was shaken to see how hard I had hit her. My hand print stayed on her bottom! My husband and I talked about this and agreed on a few rules: (1) We wouldn't hit her and she wouldn't hit us, either; (2) when her dad and I were angry, we would say; "I love you. I don't like what you just did! I still love you and will always love you."

I remember a time many years ago when I got very angry about a mess in the living room. In trying to figure out why I got so angry, I realized that I thought I had to be a "perfect" housewife in order to feel okay. I saw the mess as a sabotage of my struggle for perfection—of my attempt to be okay. Giving this a great deal of thought, I decided that I did not really believe in or want those impossible standards that I'd been trying to live up to, but I did want to feel good about myself—and my kids. I eased my standards of cleanliness to allow everyone to be more comfortable, relaxed, and happy. I also discovered other ways to develop my self-esteem.

That realization helped to stay my hand later when I wanted to punish my children. I learned to stop and think: Is a messy house a good enough reason to spank my kids? It had been for my mother, but I chose differently. My house was rarely perfect, but my kids had higher self-esteem.

Our parents raised us the only way they knew how, and we learned to parent from them. Take time to remember not only what they did to you but also its effect on you and on your relationship with them. Remember how it affected your self-esteem. For the sake of your child, let those memories return.

Our parents made mistakes, but we survived them. All parents make mistakes, but children can be remarkably resilient. Blaming only gets us stuck. It's healthier to work through a problem (therapy may be helpful), then forgive our parents and ourselves. *Learn from their mistakes, and don't repeat them.* Create the future you deserve and desire for yourself and your family. Only you can change the course of your personal history. You have the power to do it. If you need help, get it.

A friend of mine shared her story.

A battered child myself, I had no awareness of the incredible anger stored inside me until a month or so after my daughter was born. Having been raised with impatience, demands, and punishments, my instinctual behavior was to lash out whenever her needs conflicted with my limits. While in my mind I saw only love for her, I continued to hurt the most precious being in my life.

When she was one and a half, I made a conscious commitment to become the person I knew I could be, which brought me, two years later, to the realization that violation and violence had been passed down the line of women in our family, and that if I did not stop the pattern, the battering tendency would continue with my daughter. I took responsibility for making that change. It's now been twenty years, and we have created a loving, accepting, respectful, and caring relationship. A long time coming, it has definitely been worth the effort.[10]

Perhaps there is some truth in the biblical saying "The sins of the father are visited upon the third and fourth generation." Let this be the last generation. Call it quits for violence in your family. Begin, instead, a cycle of love.

"Love is the answer, whatever the question."[11]

A Course in Miracles

17

Beliefs

"Whether you believe you can or believe you can't, you're right."[1]

Henry Ford

His friends drove the high school senior home from school that autumn day. Soon afterward, he took his life. A note near his body read, "Life's a bitch, and then you die." Had this classmate of my son's had more positive beliefs, he would still be alive and enjoying his life.

Most of our beliefs are beyond our awareness. They were handed down to us from our parents, teachers, television, friends, and peers. Unquestioned, our beliefs became our truth. This truth, then, comprises our "life program," which we act out on a day-to-day basis. And as we put our beliefs into action, they become reinforced; they become real.

The beliefs people hold to be true deeply and profoundly affect who they are and what they get out of life. From our earliest decisions, we create a subconscious map that we use all our lives—even after it's outdated. Many beliefs are preverbal and beyond our awareness. For example, if young children conclude that the world is not safe, they may hold their breath to control their feelings and to numb their fear; in adulthood what may remain of this very early decision is restricted breathing in an aging body that needs all the oxygen it can get. We drag the past with us through our beliefs, expectations, attitudes, and self-talk. All these factors combine to create our reality.

What were your earliest decisions, or "truths," about life? What were your family beliefs? (Remembering the old household rules may help you to identify these beliefs.) In a way, it's easier to spend a lifetime living out hand-me-down, outdated beliefs than to uncover and examine your own life program. This is important to do, though, because otherwise you stop growing— and the beliefs you pass on to your children may not work in the world they are growing into. Become conscious of your beliefs. Allow them to enter your awareness as bubbles rise to the surface of a pond.

- What do you believe about life? Is it a rat race we must endure? Or is the universe a friendly place?
- What do you believe about children? Are they senseless little monsters who need to be tamed? Or are they exuberant beings full of life, who need to be guided?
- What do you believe about parenting? Do you believe it is a mother's duty to serve her family and a father's to earn money? Or do parents face a challenge of balancing caregiving and breadwinning in the way that's most fulfilling to each of them?

If I believe that kids are monsters, I *expect* trouble. Irritation, anger, and readiness to use punishment reflect in my *attitude*. When one of them does something I judge to be "bad," I say (*self-talk*), "It's just like him or her to do that," and I reinforce the negative *behavior*. The kid thinks (self-talk), "Mom expects me to be a holy terror," and she or he becomes one! After all, the kid doesn't want to disappoint me!

If, on the other hand, I believe my kids are precious gifts

to be loved and enjoyed, I reinforce the positive behavior. When they do something "bad," I take the time to help correct the behavior and clarify my expectations for better conduct. Again, the kids don't want to disappoint me!

Consider all the elements that create our behavior and our worldview:

Beliefs. You talk yourself into your beliefs—your truths. Your unconscious, unable to distinguish between fact and nonfact, believes whatever you tell it and then does anything and everything it can to make your truth come true. Keep an eye on your beliefs—write them out as you realize them. Then ask yourself: Do you want them to come true? Do they enhance your life? Your beliefs create your expectations.

Expectations. Once you believe something firmly, you gauge your expectations to fit your belief. Expectations are the most powerful forces in human relations. People will try to live up to expectations—their own, and those of others. Impossibly high expectations for children are among the most damaging forces there are; it means that children can never measure up. Parents are constantly disappointed and children are constantly discouraged. A child doesn't see that the standard is unrealistic, but concludes, "I'm inadequate; something's wrong with me." On the other hand, by expecting too little of children, they will conclude that parents don't believe in them; and probably won't make an effort. It's best to have high and attainable expectations. Expectations create attitudes.

Attitudes. Attitudes are habits of thought. At first we form habits; then our habits form us. Attitudes of respect or disrespect, trust or distrust, encouragement or discouragement, optimism or pessimism, color our everyday judgments.

Judgment. Often we make judgments based on out-dated beliefs, unrealistic expectations, or unforgiving attitudes. We judge others based on their jobs, their taste in clothing, and the expressions on their faces. We also judge people—usually unfairly—

based on their sex and their race. If we let our judgments get in the way (as judgments tend to do), we find ourselves dealing with our own beliefs—and not with other human beings. When we form our judgments before interacting with someone—when we prejudge—this is prejudice. When we feel the need to judge others based on our own insecurity, we need to boost our own self-esteem instead (see Chapter 3). We can become aware of our judgments by listening to our self-talk.

Self-talk. Words have great creative power; they can enhance or damage our self-esteem and the self-esteem of others. Our beliefs are enforced and repeated all the time in our thoughts with words. This is called self-talk. Self-talk, whether positive or negative, leads to behavior.

Behavior. We behave as if our beliefs are true. Our reality, the truth that we live, is a result of our beliefs. In order to change our behavior or that of our kids, therefore, we must first explore the beliefs that underpin the system; then work on changing the beliefs. Otherwise, behaviors will continue to reinforce beliefs that don't work any more.

One of the best ways to make things happen is to believe that it is so. "As you believe," taught Jesus, "so shall it be done unto you." For example, one-fourth to one-third of patients show improvement when given placebos by their physicians. Even though the pill has no active ingredients, it is powerful because the patients trust the physicians and believe they are being cured.

Young children mostly believe what the significant people in their lives tell them. If, for example, you tell a boy that he is a brat, and he believes it, he feels bratty and will probably be a brat. If a girl believes she cannot learn math, she constantly tells herself that and will counter and sabotage every positive attempt in the learning process. Children are capable of learning if they believe they can learn.

The easiest way to change people's behavior is to change their beliefs about themselves. If you believe that kids are okay and treat them accordingly, they conclude that they must be okay and become okay. If you believe that kids are smart, you expect them to be smart; they work hard to be smart because they don't want to disappoint you.

People have a variety of beliefs about life. For example, "life is a bowl of cherries," or "life is the pits." Life is to be enjoyed—or endured. You can't have everything, or you can have it all. Some beliefs are life enhancing. Others create limitations, pain, and havoc in our lives.

We look for things that prove we're right, that fit and validate our beliefs. It's called selective perception. If I believe that kids are bad, I look for things that prove I'm right. And whatever I look for, I find. In focusing on the negative, I filter out all the fun and delightful things they do. When they are helpful and do cute things, I say, "That's not like you," because it doesn't fit what I believe about them. When their behavior fits my belief, I say, "That's just like you." For better or for worse, I keep reinforcing the behavior that proves I'm right. Kids repeat the behavior that we reinforce and expect. They become what we believe they are. *What we believe is what we get.*

But rather than changing our expectations, too often we find that *we would rather be right than happy.* For example, Dad might say to Jack, "You're no good, just like your Uncle Harry." The label creates a negative expectation that Jack wants to "live up to." A self-fulfilling prophecy, Jack will tend to become like his uncle. Dad feels smug because he was "right" about the kid. Yet Jack thinks he's no good, Dad is disappointed, and everyone is miserable. Or a mother might believe that her child did something bad and may act on it, *even though it's not so.*

Examine your beliefs. What do you believe about yourself? If you know that you're valuable and competent, you expect positive relationships and achievements. Self-esteem is believing that you are a worthwhile person. The higher your self-esteem, the higher your expectations (short of expecting "perfection").

If you believe that you are the scum of the earth, you'll expect very little of and for yourself. The lower your self-esteem, the lower your expectations. And *you get in life what you believe you deserve.*

When something isn't working in their lives, people seldom do search for the real source of the problem and unravel the underlying cause. Yet this is what we must do with the beliefs that limit our lives and harm our relationships. Life changes. People change. Society changes. Beliefs also change. What was valid when you were a child or an adolescent may no longer be valid in today's world.

Examine your hand-me-down beliefs, and keep only those that enhance your life. Get rid of the ones that are damaging or no longer make sense. Our beliefs are too powerful to be ignored. Our health and happiness depend on making positive, conscious choices. Our future depends on it.

18

Self-Talk

"All that we are is the result of what we have thought."[1]

The Buddha

I used to stalk wild asparagus in the spring. Equipped with a pillowcase and a tiny pocket knife, I set out every four or five days looking for new shoots. One beautiful day, I discovered some luscious stalks just begging to be picked—on the wrong side of a barbed wire fence. I tried to resist the temptation but. . . .

While harvesting my new asparagus patch, I became aware of someone approaching me. Turning, I saw an older man with a little brown bag—and a great big butcher knife! I stood, smiled weakly, and gulped. The man mumbled something about "territory," making me a little nervous. Trying to change the subject, I introduced myself and asked him to tell me about himself. Mr. Miller had grown up there, and as a kid he used to ice skate for miles on the frozen ditch. He'd never married and lived alone at the edge of town. In an effort to make a graceful exit before he could bring up territory again, I invited him to join my family for a steak and asparagus dinner. He smiled and said, "Much obliged, ma'am, but I don't mix well."

His words echoed in my mind as I walked home. He had probably said "I don't mix well" thousands, if not millions, of times throughout his life—to himself and to others. He had let me in on some of his self-talk. And of course, he didn't show up for dinner.

Mr. Miller sees himself as shy—perhaps as a social misfit. This ties into his self-talk, his feelings, and his behavior. The pattern probably began years ago. Perhaps he overheard an off-hand remark from a significant person. Perhaps he was told over and over as a child that he was clumsy and stupid, and learned to believe that people wouldn't like him if he tried to "mix." Perhaps once he had a tragic experience that made him accept himself as a loner.

From the countless experiences of our lives we observe situations and draw our personal conclusions and truths. This internal dialogue, or *self-talk*, reflects our beliefs and creates our *feelings*. We express our feelings through our *behavior*, which then reinforces our *self-concept*. Self-talk, thus, is self-fulfilling.

If you repeated "I don't mix well" over and over to yourself, without anyone to tell you any different, what would you feel? Lonely, lacking in confidence, low in self-esteem? How would you behave? Might you be awkward, withdrawn, isolated? Self-talk reflects our self-concept or beliefs about ourselves and about life; it creates feelings that we express through our behavior. Finally, our behavior reinforces our self-concept.

Self-concept. Self-concept is simply the belief we have of ourselves at any given moment. It changes as we change. Many people have a mistaken idea of self-concept. Janet might say, "I was shy when I was born, I'm shy today, and I'll be shy the day I die." Janet is stuck.

Self-image is how we imagine ourselves to be—what we can be and how others see us. Our self-image determines our performance. A negative self-image automatically sets up a failure mechanism. A positive self-image sets up a success mechanism.

Self-talk. We talk to ourselves all the time. Self-talk refers to the most important and powerful inner voice that we hear, either in our thoughts or *beneath* them. It controls our beliefs, our self-image, our self-concept, and ultimately, our self-esteem.

One winter when I was skiing, for example, I fell every time the trail was steep. I noticed that just before I fell, I'd say, "I'm going to fall." I decided to flip my self-talk, and said, "I'm doing great!" That affirmation encouraged me and changed my attitude. I maneuvered down the hill like a pro.

Self-talk prescribes our self-esteem. With our self-talk, we plant in our unconscious what will grow in our lives. We either encourage or discourage ourselves; we lift ourselves up or put ourselves down; we empower or victimize ourselves. The quality of self-talk determines whether we are our own best friend or our worst enemy. Only when we tune in and listen to the old messages from the past can we begin to free ourselves of their grip on our present life.

Remember the slogan we heard when computers first appeared: "Garbage in, garbage out" (GIGO). If you baked a gingerbread cake with ingredients such as dust, mustard, and small sharp nails, it wouldn't come out of the oven smelling warm and spicy and wonderful like gingerbread should. Likewise, if a lot of garbage has found its way into your mind, it probably spills negativity into your life.

When your self-esteem drops, listen to what you're saying to yourself. The reason most people have low self-esteem is that they keep telling themselves how awful they are. People who were blamed and criticized a lot as children tend to replay those negative statements—"stinkin' thinking"—over and over again, like endlessly looping cassette tapes. Often the volume of the internal dialogue is so low that people aren't aware of it. Turn up the volume. What do you hear? Write it down. Do you like what you hear? What would you do if someone else said those things to you?

Once you know what you say to yourself, you are free to make changes. *With awareness comes choice.* You can continue to repeat those messages or make a new tape and create new experiences.

Feelings. Our self-talk affects our feelings. Imagine yourself saying over and over, "I'm a loser." As you worry that you might fail, you create feelings of failure: discouragement, defeat, and depression. You keep yourself from taking any risks whatsoever, and stagnate. Now, let that go. Say to yourself several times instead, "I'm a winner." Your thoughts about winning and succeeding create winning feelings: encouragement, motivation, and excitement. When you can use those feelings to confront the negative ones, you'll find you have less fear of expressing your desires and intentions.

Behavior. Our behavior is a reflection of how we feel about ourselves. We tend to act out feelings—with words or behavior. If we feel like winners, we act like winners—working hard, thinking clearly, and doing what we need to do to win. If we feel like losers, we act like losers and become losers. Our behaviors reinforce our self-concept—seeing ourselves as either winners or losers. Over time, we tend to become what we think about the most.

I remember a woman who cried herself to sleep every night because she thought she was a "bad" mother. That thought created feelings (guilt, sadness, and anger), that led to behavior (crying every night), that affected her self-concept—and her ability to be with her child. Instead of beating herself up, she could change her self-talk. Instead of discouraging herself, she could substitute encouraging affirmations instead. She might say, "I am a loving and effective mother" twenty or thirty times each day. It might feel like a lie at first, but would get easier and more believable. The positive self-talk would alter her feelings about herself, and her behavior and self-concept would reflect the difference.

It can be helpful to trace troublesome thoughts to the source and determine if there is any truth in them, then deal with and heal them. Learn from mistakes and change your behavior. Ask for forgiveness and forgive yourself. Then use positive self-talk to support positive changes. We can give ourselves messages that reinforce the negative—or that affirm the positive in our lives and help bring it about. Affirmations empower us to change our thinking—and our lives.

"Stinkin' Thinking"

There are some patterns of "stinkin' thinking" that we all share—games we play with our minds that keep us stuck in a win-lose mindset. We need to learn to catch ourselves in the act with these faulty habits, and laugh at our assumptions.

• In **polarized (either-or) thinking**,[2] there is no gray area, no middle ground. We are either good or bad, perfect or a failure. As a result, emotions swing dramatically from one extreme to the other. Because of one little flaw, we become totally worthless.

The Alternative: Watch for either-or, black-white judgments. When you catch yourself doing that, ask how the opposite is also true. If, for example, you hear yourself saying, "The house is a total mess," look for parts of the house that are not messy. Realize that, with 1 or 10 thinking, you are blocking out 2 through 9. Lower your expectations and look for the gray areas that make up most of our experience.

• In **personalization**, we take everything personally, even when it isn't personal. For example, I might see someone scowling and conclude that she is scowling at me. At dinner, if I make broccoli and someone doesn't like it, I might conclude that something's wrong with me, and feel hurt.

The Alternative: If it isn't personal, don't take it personally. Check out your assumptions. Ask questions. Maybe she always scowls! Maybe someone had a bad experience with broccoli once! Detach yourself from the situation for a moment: It most likely has nothing to do with you or your personal worth. If a kid makes a mess, and mother says, "How could you do that to me?"—maybe she should consider the more likely possibility: The kid made the mess for himself or herself, without a thought of hurting Mother. Parents need to separate themselves from their children so they don't take kids' behavior personally. The higher our own self-esteem, the easier it is to avoid such reactions.

• In **projection**, or mindreading, we project on to others what is going on in our own self-talk. Did you ever wear a shirt with a spot on it and imagine that everyone you spoke to was staring at it critically? Have you ever been sure that the reason a friend hasn't called (or written) is because he or she was mad at you, when they weren't? Or have you been in an argument with a friend or lover, and accused him or her of the very things you discovered yourself feeling—five minutes later?

The Alternative: When you catch yourself projecting your thoughts, do a reality check. If your self-talk thinks your friend is judging you on your messy house, try to prove it. Is she eyeing everything critically? Is she wearing white gloves? Or is she looking right at you smiling—happy to see you? Chances are it's a fabrication of your own faulty thinking. Your negative feelings (guilt, anger, rejection) may be the result of your own thinking (self-talk) and have nothing to do with your visitor. And listen carefully to the words that come out of your mouth. They may hold a message for you.

• When **catastrophizing**, we imagine and expect the worst. A headache is a sure sign of a brain tumor; a minor financial setback means we'll starve to death, for sure. Any little thing may be a sign of impending doom. These days it's easy to do, as the news brings us new reasons to panic every day; with catastrophizing, we can put ourselves into a total panic that devastates our sense of well-being.

The Alternative: Mark Twain remarked, "I've had many worries in my life, and most of them never came to pass." Consider the odds against your conclusion—the brain tumor, starvation. Don't make a mountain out of a molehill. Think of the many times you imagined the worst and were wrong. Do you want to keep doing it? Disaster is always a remote possibility, but never very probable. Trust life and remember the saying, "God never gives us more than we can handle."

• In **blaming**, we find fault either in ourselves or in others. We either assume total responsibility for everything that goes wrong ("What's wrong with me?") or we accept no personal responsibility for difficulties and put it all on others. We point a blaming finger at everyone else or beat our breast in guilt.

The Alternative: We are all responsible for our own behavior and its consequences. In relationships, both persons are responsible for creating a problem—and for creating a solution. Listen for the words blame and fault and get rid of them. Instead, think in terms of accepting responsibility—and sharing it. Go for no-fault communication. Only then can you solve problems and move ahead.

• In **overgeneralization**, if something bad has happened to us once, we expect it to happen again. Limited situations lead to absolute conclusions. For example, you make one mistake, like botching an important test in junior high, and you conclude that you're no good at math. When visiting my future mother-in-law years ago, I discovered that there was no toilet paper on the bathroom roll. I concluded that moment that she was an "awful housekeeper." If you notice that one thing is wrong, and another thing, you leap to the conclusion that everything is wrong—all the time. You may even talk yourself into believing that it's bad now, it always was, and it always will be—forever and ever, amen.

The Alternative: First of all, be aware of what you are doing. Then, examine the evidence for your conclusion and the evidence against it. Weigh your information. (It took me a long time to realize what a precious contribution that "awful housekeeper" made to our family—t.p. or no. Her gifts were of laughter and fishing and sauerkraut chocolate cake. "Makes it moist," she said.) Also listen for "big" words: never, always, everybody, nobody. Use them only with great care—or when you're joking.

• **Having to be right** all the time puts you into conflict with everyone whose viewpoint differs. It makes people hard of hearing. When others differ with you, you ignore them or feel compelled to prove them wrong. You find yourself in more power struggles than you would like. Minor differences seem major because self-esteem and personal worth are at stake. When reality differs from the way you think it should be, you deny it. Having to be right all the time makes people lonely.

The Alternative: Reality is not the way we want it to be—reality is the way it is. We need to remove the blinders and see what really is, instead of trying to force the world to fit our personal image of how it's supposed to be. In our culture, people have many different perceptions, experiences, and lifestyles. There are many different "right" ways. It would be a dull world if there was only one right way. And whose right way would be accepted as right by everyone else? (If it wasn't yours, could you be happy?) We must each find what's best for ourselves—what is right—and allow others to do the same.

Affirmations

Imagine, for a moment, a blue hippo. Now, *don't* think of a blue hippo!

How did you get rid of the blue hippo? You probably thought of something else—maybe a red hippo or a green giraffe or a flower. To get rid of the first image, most people replace it with another. And that is exactly how we must work with our unconscious to make important changes in our lives. *Think about— affirm—what you want in order to get rid of what you don't want.*

With affirmations we talk back to negative self-talk. We reprogram ourselves and create the kind of transformation we felt when we learned to ride a bicycle or swim. We can move from "I can't" to "Of course I can!" We no longer have to be controlled by our past. Affirmations help us believe in the good things we want and expect for ourselves. We can substitute positive messages to expel the garbage from our minds and to heal the damage caused by years of negative thinking.

We can also use affirmations to counter put-downs. When someone tells eleven-year-old Frank that he's stupid, he can correct it in his self-talk saying, "That's not true. I'm good at math."

Now close your eyes and imagine someone very special entering the room, walking up behind you, gently touching your shoulders, and whispering something important about you that you've been wanting to hear. Listen. Those whispered words may be the perfect affirmation for you. Rephrase them in the form, "I am ____." You can be your own best friend and give this message to yourself instead of hoping and wishing for someone else to say it to you. Every morning, when you look in the mirror, you can say, "I accept and love you just the way you are." You can also say, "I am creating my life exactly as I want it." Repeat such affirmations twenty to thirty times every day, allowing the positive feelings to flow, little by little, until you believe yourself, until you become your real self.

This process makes more sense once we understand the nature of the unconscious: It can't tell the difference between fact and fiction, between what's imagined and what's real. *The unconscious will believe anything we tell it and will do everything it can to make that happen.* As with a fertile garden, whatever we plant in our unconscious will grow. If we plant carrots, we won't get petunias; and if we plant nothing, we'll probably get weeds.

What are the seeds for the unconscious? The thoughts we think (self-talk) and the pictures we imagine. "Imagination is everything," said Albert Einstein. "It is the preview of life's coming attractions." What we see is what we get. Also, the words we repeat over and over in our minds have great power; eventually they become our reality. *We become what we think about the most.*

If your children tell you they can't do something, help them turn it around saying, "Let's pretend that you can!" And be sure to read that wonderful story *The Little Engine that Could*. That little engine knew how to use affirmations to achieve greatness. Self-talk is especially important to learning-disabled children, who get many negative messages from themselves and others. Encouragement, patience, and real skills to compensate for their differences are important, but positive self-talk is what makes these things stick.

A child with positive self-talk and high self-esteem is one who will demonstrate positive behavior that reinforces the positive self-talk. On the other hand, a child with negative self-talk and low self-esteem will exhibit negative behavior that reinforces the negative self-talk. Whatever you can do to build your child's self-esteem will pay off in a happier child with more positive behavior.

You can direct your thoughts. When you accept responsibility for your self-talk, you take charge of your self-esteem. *By changing your mind, you can change your life.*

19

Obsession
with Perfection

"A perfectionist is someone who takes great pains . . . and gives them to others."[1]

Anonymous

I had to be a perfect hostess. I had to cook a perfect meal and set a perfect table, with no wrinkles in the tablecloth. The house had to look perfect. I had to look perfect. When the doorbell rang, I had to be calm and smiling and beautiful, as though I'd done nothing all day long; I'd be stressed out worrying about details and neglecting my own agendas, but I'd never show it. I was what I thought a perfect wife should be. But I don't remember ever really enjoying myself or my guests.

When I realized how much my perfectionist expectations were inhibiting my lifestyle and cramping my self-expression, I decided to make some major changes. I gave myself permission to attempt things I never thought I could do and enjoy myself more. In doing so, I have taken more risks, made more mistakes, and gained more wisdom. Free from the vice of perfectionism, life is much more fun and a lot easier.

Women are tempted by many sources to believe that unless they are perfect they won't find or hang onto a man; and men often buy into this. It doesn't happen that way. The problem begins when children conclude that only if they are perfect will their parents love them. If parents withhold acceptance and affection, children have to earn it. They work harder and harder to be accepted, to be loved, to be okay. The ultimate hope of this ongoing struggle is that they will be accepted, approved of, and loved unconditionally—just for being themselves.

The media, Hollywood, and magazines bombard all of us, women in particular, with expectations of perfection. So may our peers. It is important to have high standards for ourselves, but it's too easy to obsess on being what we think we *should* be—perfect. Striving to be a perfect wife with a Jane Fonda body, a perfect mother with honor-roll children, and a Julia Child cook serving gourmet dinners sets one up for chronic disappointment, dissatisfaction, and exhaustion. Only when we do things absolutely perfectly do we think we are okay. One widow confessed that she even felt she had to grieve perfectly! These popular cultural pressures are so pervasive it's hard to escape them.

Always looking for something wrong, perfectionists find it, then are shocked and angry about it. They have unrealistic or impossible expectations: Only perfection will do. Yet, human beings can't be perfect for very long. Just one failing, fault, or flaw proves what perfectionists believe deep down—that they are total failures. This either/or thinking—being either a 10 or a 0—allows no middle ground. They are either all good or all bad. Mistakes, therefore, are terrifying. The gray area—1 through 9—is missing. One perfectionist was actually told by her mother, "You are perfect or you are nothing."

Those who have difficulty accepting themselves have difficulty accepting others. Those who are judgmental and critical of themselves tend to be judgmental and critical of their spouses, children, and friends. And, while good at giving criticism, they fear it from others and easily become defensive. They fight to be right because they can't stand the thought of being wrong, inevitably resulting in conflicts. Under pressure to be perfect, they keep up a façade of perfection. Playing this role while knowing that it is phony creates absolute stress and can tear them up inside.

Decision making produces intense anxiety for perfectionists because they want to make a perfect decision. They may procrastinate in doing tasks, or avoid finishing them; after all, if they don't start or don't finish, they can avoid being judged. In business settings they waste immeasurable amounts of time and materials at high costs to the company; they can spend hours writing one letter.

Many children feel the pressure to be perfect. Getting up to bat can be terrifying when you believe that you have to hit the ball every time it crosses the plate. The tension is intensified if a perfectionist parent is watching. Kids might quit or may not even bother to try. If they don't try, they reason, they can't fail.

The thought of making their bed or cleaning their bedroom can strike them with terror, discouragement, and despair. One thirteen-year-old boy, after spending many hours cleaning his room called his dad in to inspect it. Dad glanced around the room, stroked the wall and said, "You didn't oil the paneling." He might have been kidding, but the praise the child deserved was buried under the flip response. Everyone connected with a perfectionist suffers from low self-esteem.

Perfectionists may end up doing all the work themselves because no one else can do it "just right," which means perfect. They suffer, therefore, from chronic fatigue and stress. When they do successfully complete a task, they never give themselves a pat on the back because they are busy looking for flaws. A perfectionist, for example, who raises $80,000 for his or her favorite charity might say, "It should have been $100,000." They don't see the success and savor it; they only see how it wasn't good enough.

Child perfectionists with straight A's have killed themselves when they received their first B. A similar story is that of Ludwig Boltzmann, considered to be one of the twenty greatest physicists of all time. Acclaimed as one of the principal founders of statistical mechanics, he himself was never quite satisfied with his work, and finally took his own life. His perfectionist perceptions prevented him from feeling content with his outstanding achievements. Perfectionism can be deadly, both psychologically and physically.

Many teenage girls are often obsessed with perfection. Bombarded with images of perfection presented by the media, they may feel inadequate because they can never keep up with all the latest trends and styles. They can suffer constant conflict with their self-image, while trying to live up to being a perfect woman. In other words, their self-esteem suffers. Girls who reject sex-role stereotyping, however, tend to have a stronger sense of self-esteem. Rather than comparing themselves to unattainable standards, they focus on and appreciate their own intrinsic values.[2]

Perfectionist parents focus on surface qualities. They invest in a façade of perfection, based on an image/ideal/fantasy of how they think a child is supposed to be. A pimple, a spot on the shirt, or unruly hair command their attention to such a degree that they may not hear what a kid is experiencing. They may miss their child's feelings, concerns, struggles, growth, and inner beauty. Perfectionists may be stunted in their development due to confusion and anxiety, stemming from lack of appreciation and support.

No human being is perfect. Anyone who has a body or a kitchen knows that there is no such thing as perfection—at least not for long! There is no such thing as a perfect man, a perfect woman, a perfect child, or a perfect couple. "Perfect" media models endure starvation, bulimia, and cosmetic surgery to get that way. If all else fails to remove or coverup wrinkles, moles, pimples, fat, and grey hair, photographs of them are airbrushed to remove every last flaw. We compare ourselves to the manufactured pictures of models and then think that something is wrong with us. (See Chapter 20.)

Of the thousands of participants in my workshops who are striving to be perfect, no one has achieved it. All their lives they've worked so that one day they would be really okay, which, to a perfectionist, means perfect.

It's no fun being a perfectionist. Perfectionism robs us of joy, playful abandon, utter relaxation and spontaneity. Perfectionism is a compulsion that may predispose people to depression, alcoholism, eating disorders, and obsessive-compulsive behaviors. Perfectionism also takes time and energy away from families. When children grow up, their warmest memories will not be of how clean the house was, but of the time the family has spent together.

Here are several tips for recovering from perfectionism:

• **Admit that you're only human.** It is our privilege as human beings to be imperfect! Some even say it's our duty. Turkish carpetmakers weave flaws into their design, reasoning that only God is perfect! In this culture, it takes courage to allow ourselves to be imperfect. Yet, when we accept our imperfections and forgive ourselves, we are able to accept and forgive others.

Who said that parents always have to be right? When we accept ourselves completely—including the fact that we are fallible—the burden lightens. It's a relief not to have to be perfect—not to have to play God.

Admit your mistakes. You can simply state, "Yesterday I said (or did) such-and-such and I realize today that I was wrong." Kids know how human they are; when you share your flaws with them, it gives them hope—and builds a bond between you.

• **Turn mistakes into teachers.** If it is human to err, then children are very human. They are always losing, forgetting, or spilling things. When they cry over spilled milk, just ask them to clean it up and be more careful next time. Self-esteem sags when children make mistakes; when they fix them, they regain their self-esteem. Help them to figure out what went wrong, so they can avoid a repeat performance. A mistake, after all, is just one way that didn't work.

A friend of mine went through a series of unhealthy relationships before noticing that she was making the same moves each time with the same type of man. As soon as she realized this, her "luck" began to change and she suddenly met a man with whom she could be herself.

In doing, risking, and trying new things, we develop judgment skills. We learn how to evaluate, how to analyze, how to determine what old information transfers to new situations. A person who makes mistakes gains wisdom. Thomas Edison made thousands of mistakes; he was also granted more than 1,000 patents. Failure can breed success. There is no successful person, living or dead, who has not failed many, many times. Success is learned and earned. Viewing mistakes as learning opportunities is a life-saving and life-enhancing skill. People who learn to learn from mistakes gain confidence, competence, and judgment skills.

• **Laugh at your mistakes.** Share them with family and friends. One mom told me that they play Bloopers at the dinner table. Mom and Dad begin with stories of their daily blunders, and each kid follows.

After filling my gas tank one time, for example, I went through the car wash. It was only when I turned onto the street and heard a clunk did I realize that I had not put the gas cap back on. I spent the rest of the afternoon with my mechanic trying to figure out how to get rid of the soapy water without sacrificing the tank of gas. At home, everyone laughed at my mistake. My kids learned from it and will never repeat it—nor will I.

Blooper time is a fun time, since the whole family has a

chance to laugh with each other, at each other, and at them-selves—and then get on with life. It can lighten up life for everyone in the family.

• **Reorder your priorities.** One mother of three preschool children vacuumed the carpet three times each day. I suggested that she rethink this. The following week she reported that she had cut back to twice a day. "No one seemed to notice," she said, "and I had more time for my children." Do you want to be a slave to household perfection? A perfect house is impossible with chil-dren. "When all else fails," a wise person said, "lower your expec-tations." Stop trying to be Superwoman or Superman. "Simplify, simplify, simplify," wrote Henry David Thoreau. Translated, this means to create an easier lifestyle for yourself. There are merits in messiness; it means life is filled with more important and fun things than housework. Design a family life that is healthier and more enjoyable for everyone.

Life is short; examine your priorities. What's really impor-tant in your life? Good parenting? Go for excellence in that area. Be the best that you can be! In other areas, such as planting a garden, "good enough" will do just fine. Beet seeds do not have to be in a straight line exactly one-half inch deep and three-quarters of an inch apart. Do you really want to spend three days getting them in just right? Make yourself a sign and hang it on your refrigerator: "Nothing is perfect and it's all OKAY!"

• **Stop the stinkin' thinking that says "I'm not good enough."** Listen to whose voice it is that tells you that. Then realize that it was *only an opinion* at a moment in time based on *someone's* perfectionist expectations. The fact is, *you are good enough and always have been!* Change the nagging, damaging message that keeps telling you differently. Try these affirmations.

"I am good enough."
"I am not perfect, but I am okay."
"I don't have to be perfect; I like myself just the way I am."

Repeat these affirmations a few times. They may feel strange at first, but that perception will change. Over time, these sayings will heal you and help you to transcend perfectionism. Meanwhile, celebrate your achievements. List your successes, acknowledge them, and celebrate them.

• **Be gentle with yourself.** It's fine to want to have a nice table set for a dinner party, but spending an hour folding and refolding napkins, ironing and reironing the tablecloth, is problematic. Relax. Breathe deeply. Be flexible. Focus on and enjoy the experience of life rather than the accomplishment of it.

• **Put more spontaneity, silliness, and joy into your life.** Kids can teach you how to play. (If you don't have any, borrow some!) When you pick up your child from daycare, stop at a park to unwind and reconnect. Roll down a grassy hill, go down a slide, skip rope. Pretend. Children can help you make a fool of yourself, and it might be the best thing for you. When you laugh and play together, stress goes down and self-esteem goes up. As you create rich memories, you'll nudge yourself beyond the obsession with perfection.

> You can't be a friend unless you are yourself.
> You can't be yourself until you know yourself.
> You can't know yourself unless you admit your mistakes.
> You can't admit your mistakes if you're pretending to be perfect.
> And you can't be perfect—because you're human.
> Enjoy it! Celebrate it!

R E L A X

20

Cultural Barriers to Self-Esteem

"The first problem for all of us, men and women, is not to learn, but to unlearn."[1]

Gloria Steinem

Self-esteem is as important to our well-being as legs are to a table. It is essential for physical and mental health and for happiness. Given its importance, everyone should be taught skills for self-esteem development. Instead, we are more often taught ideas and behaviors that lower self-esteem—our own and that of our children.

Young children have amazing memories. By nature, they are very impressionable because they have so much to learn to prepare themselves for the rest of life. Ready and eager to learn about their world and how to be in it, they take in everything. Naturally trusting, they believe what they are taught, accepting it as the "truth" about how the world is. The "truth" that they learn shapes their behavior.

In simpler cultures this works very well. From parents and others who care about them, children learn what they need to know to become effective adults. In our culture things are different; children learn less from their preoccupied parents, little from caring neighbors, and too much from Hollywood and Madison Avenue. As a result, they miss out on the essential life skills they need to become healthy and competent adults. Our mass-media cultural myths and values clutter their minds—and ours—with misinformation that can be a prison of frustration, dissatisfaction, alienation, and pain.

From an unhealthy society and dysfunctional families, children learn dysfunctional patterns of relating to others. According to authors Barry and Janae Weinhold, codependency is responsible for most human misery "Codependency is learned dysfunctional behavior and is the result of the failure to complete one or more of the important developmental tasks during early childhood," and occurs in about 98 percent of the adult population.[2]

Some major symptoms of codependency are

- low self-esteem
- being a people pleaser and approval seeker
- feeling like a martyr
- having poorly defined psychological boundaries
- seeking outside stimulation (alcohol, food, work, or sex, for example) as a distraction from feelings
- feeling addicted to and trapped in damaging relationships, and powerless to change them
- being unable to express love and true intimacy

Any one of these characteristics can create problems for individuals. Combined with others, they create a trap for parents and children alike. Recovery comes with unraveling what doesn't work and replacing it with what does work.

It takes courage and a lot of time to begin to find one's own set of beliefs and values. I spent many years sifting through what I had learned early in my life, unraveling the misinformation, poking holes in my myths, peeling off the layers of my beliefs. I had to unlearn what didn't work, then relearn what did. At age forty, I felt that I finally knew what I needed to know at fourteen.

Perfectionism is an extremely common stumbling block to self-esteem (see Chapter 19). There are many other related barriers to self-esteem and mental health that our culture constructs. Because Western civilization has long been influenced by patriarchal values, many of them apply more to women than to men. These barriers can be deadly—either psychologically (draining our life force), or physically (resulting in illness and suicide), but they *can* be overcome with awareness, attention, new choices, and dedication to self-empowerment. The payoff of tearing down these barriers is an easier, more fulfilling life.

Self Put-Downs

In high school, I once told a friend that I thought I had a nice smile. She responded that I was conceited and shouldn't toot my own horn! I had a little talk with myself and concluded that it was not okay to say good things about myself in this world. Later on, if I ever had the nerve to again mention my smile, I'd make sure to humble myself; "I have a nice smile—but I have lots of cavities."

Many people, women in particular, learn that it is not acceptable to publicly pat themselves on the back. When they do, they are criticized for bragging. So they learn to put themselves down instead. Doing that, their self-esteem suffers.

Will Rogers said, "If it's the truth, it can't be bragging." No one achieves greatness by being self-deprecating. Scientists and soccer players, mothers and musicians, become great by acknowledging their strengths, believing in themselves, and working hard for their personal goals. After setting a goal, they find encouragement and support from others, and take pride in their progress.

The word pride is used both positively—"I'm proud of you"—and negatively—"Don't be proud." To me, to be proud means to feel good about someone and/or their performance. On the other hand, to make one-up/one-down comparisons— "I'm great and you're not"—is false pride or egotism. Feeling good at someone else's expense is not healthy.

Listen to what you say to yourself. Look into a mirror and tune in to your self-talk. Are you saying, "Boy, are *you* ugly/fat/ dumb!" If a friend talked to you like that, how would you feel? Instead, say something nice to yourself. Whisper "sweet nothings" in your own ear. And tell other people the good things about yourself. Most people really *do* prefer to hear the positive things about you and your life rather than the negative things.

Begin also to listen closely to how you talk to your children. Listen for, then ban, negativity; it lowers self-esteem Look for the good intentions in stupid behavior, and acknowledge them. Catch your kids being good and appreciate them. This will make them more aware of their positive attributes and raise their self-esteem. Being positive is also more fun than being negative!

Listen to how your children talk about themselves. Negative statements, such as "I'm so dumb" or "I never do anything right," let you know what they are repeating over and over again to themselves. The negative self-talk leads to negative feelings and negative behavior.

To counter this, you might introduce the Eleventh Commandment: "Thou shalt not speak negatively of thyself or others." Establish a rule that every negative statement is to be countered with two positive statements. This will help you become aware of how you talk to yourself—and about others—and will flip the focus to the positive.

Look for the good qualities in yourself and in your kids. Ask them to tell you what they like about themselves. Sit down with them and encourage them to talk about how they're special. Get them to start learning to think positively about themselves.

Parents and teachers alike report that kids love doing this, and their self-esteem increases instantly.

Self-Sacrifice

In our culture (and in many others), women tend to be defined as caretakers of everyone's needs but their own. Women have learned to expect and hope that by doing enough caretaking, their turn will come automatically; but somehow, it rarely does. Women are still led to believe that taking care of themselves is "selfish." (Jewish mothers get the stereotype for this, but we all do it!) "I almost denied myself out of existence," confessed one woman who was taught to be self-negating. Many become long-suffering martyrs and doormats, watching life pass them by. Emotionally bankrupt, many burn out.

Those who never stand up for their own preferences or rights, however, can be very annoying and a burden to others. Take the classic example of a friend's grandmother who was invited to tour San Francisco in a convertible. If she sat in the passenger's seat, she could enjoy the view without too much wind, and her grown grandchildren could sit in the back and enjoy a windy, gorgeous ride. She refused to take the front seat, though, insisting she was being treated too well. Consequently, the top stayed up. She couldn't appreciate the exciting views, and no one had a good time By taking the back seat and trying not to inconvenience anyone, she inconvenienced everyone

After having two babies eleven months apart, I wish someone had told me to take care of myself and get plenty of exercise and rest. I wish someone had given me permission to play more. I wish someone had told me that naptime for baby is "self-time" for mom. Mothers have to take care of themselves so they can take care of others. Self-care is the primary issue, because you can't give what you haven't got

The last part of Jesus' only commandment states that *we*

must love our neighbors as ourselves. Self-love comes first. The best thing you can do for your kids is to be good and loving to yourself. Take good care of yourself for your own sake and for your children's.

"Kids' needs are best met by grownups whose needs are met," writes Jean Illsley Clarke.[3] Yet there are times when we need to put our own needs on hold, especially with young children. One of the challenges of parenting is to do for our kids *and* for ourselves. We need to strike a healthy balance in which no one comes out losing.

It is okay and necessary to relax and take time for yourself. It's also important to take time for your friends, for your spouse. You entered a relationship to be friends, to be lovers, to have fun together. Often, when kids come along, parents fall out of touch with each other. It's important to nurture and enrich your relationship with your mate; that's where it all started. One day, when your kids are grown, you will be alone with each other again. The love that exists between parents showers down on the children. Being in the presence of two people who truly love and support each other has a powerful positive effect on children. All important relationships need to be nurtured.

Be good to yourself . . . you deserve it! When you are good to yourself, you feel good about yourself. This is called self-care. It's important that you take good care of yourself because you can't give what you haven't got. *Take good care of yourself because your children are counting on you to take good care of them!*

Always Pleasing Others

Many people are taught to spend their lives trying to please others. They never say no, for fear of displeasing someone or making someone mad at them. Because they were raised seeking acceptance, they became people pleasers, begging for crumbs of approval from others. They smile all the time, hoping that everyone will like them and enjoy being with them. These people never feel really okay; they suffer from low self-esteem.

Here's a message for people pleasers: The person most important for you to please is yourself. Think of a time you prepared a nice meal for someone and worked hard on it, but something wasn't quite right. Afterward, someone gave you a compliment—"That was delicious!" What did you do with their remark? Not being pleased yourself, you probably discounted it or ignored it because you didn't believe it. In fact, if the whole world had stood up and thanked you, and you were not pleased yourself, you probably would not have noticed the applause! You must first be pleased before you can let in the appreciation and recognition of others. Then, if someone does give you a compliment, it is icing on the cake.

As a senior in high school, I was voted "the most cheerful" person in a class of three hundred girls. Wanting to be pleasing so that everyone would like me, I wore a permanent smile, which actually had little to do with cheer. I was shocked in graduate school to learn that statistically one out of eight people would not like me (or anyone else)!

Struggling with this, I learned that little girls are socialized to want to be liked by others, while boys are socialized to look for respect. I realized that, if being liked is most important, people will do anything to achieve it—even things that are against their principles. It's a vulnerable position that invites manipulation (for example, "If you don't do ____, I won't like you"). People pleasers lack the inner strength to "just say no." Young girls, consequently, who want to be pleasing to others are easy victims of "date rape."

After giving this lots of thought, I decided that I would rather have people respect me than like me. I stopped smiling all the time. I began to respect myself more, and others began to respect me more. My self-esteem moved up many notches as my definitions of what pleased *me* changed.

Assuming Too Much Responsibility for Other People's Lives

When babies are born, parents have total responsibility for their survival and well-being. As they grow and are able to do things for themselves, parents must turn over more and more responsibility to them—from feeding themselves to driving themselves—thereby lightening their own load.

If this transfer does not occur, if parents carry more responsibility than is necessary or appropriate, children are deprived of opportunities to grow, develop, and expand. If women believe that mothering is their only role, they may keep the responsibility of caretaking longer than necessary—and thus deprive their children of their own self-responsibility. Parents who carry too much responsibility may feel burdened and try to control others. Blame and anger often result, with everyone's self-esteem dropping. Likewise, women often find themselves trying to "mother" their partners. Adults should be parents to children, not to other adults.

This assumption of too much responsibility can be particularly heavy for parents whose children have special needs. All too often parents continue to do things that the child was capable of taking over long ago. Your children are whole and complete. Share with them the vision that they will be able to take over the responsibilites in their own life, even if they will always need some extra support.

We can't remind ourselves often enough that every person is first and foremost responsible for himself or herself. The task of the parent shifts from having total responsibility over infants to having almost no responsibility over them as adults. The task of the child shifts from having no responsibility as an infant to having total responsibility as an adult. This gradual letting-go process, in harmony with the developmental stages of the child, occurs over a fifteen- to twenty-year period.

We all remember the delight of a youngster saying, "Look

at me! I can do it all by myself!" We say, "Good for you! Now you can put on your own shoes." We release some responsibility.

We teach children responsibility by teaching ourselves not to do things for them that they can do for themselves. Teach them new skills to lighten your load. Encourage them to participate as team players and praise their contribution. Learn to delegate. Recognize, however, that there is more than one way to do things; allow children to express their individuality in completing tasks.

As they learn to do more and more things for themselves, their competence and confidence increase. As children assume more responsibility for their behavior and their lives, we parents can relax our protectiveness, trust them more, and breathe a sigh of relief as our responsibility lightens. Then we can refocus and get on with other important areas in our own lives.

Our Bodies Are Never Okay

Most women think that something is wrong with their bodies. They compare themselves to the current "perfect" body type, put themselves down, and feel bad. Like fashions, the ideal figure keeps shifting. The *Playboy* centerfold body, for example, is five pounds lighter than it was a few years ago. Perfect body types go in and out of style—yet our bodies stay basically the same.

The cultural stereotype for women's bodies is not only damaging, it is also absurd. In a recent book, Jane Fonda discusses becoming bulimic in high school. "For several of us at my school," she writes, "it was the beginning of a nightmarish addiction that would undermine our lives for decades to come."[4] She, and many of us, became obsessed with an external ideal, rather than concentrating on the person inside.

Bulimia, anorexia, and other eating disorders have reached epidemic proportions. Little girls nine and ten years old are dieting because their mothers are—when they should be having a wonderful time climbing trees, riding bikes, and exploring the world. They have internalized the cultural value that they must have a "perfect" (skinny) body in order to be acceptable; they are not okay as they are. As women take in these cultural messages, many have learned to hate their bodies and reject themselves.

The obsession with physical perfection is not a personal problem, but rather a social issue. Many women get discouraged and resort to drastic measures to match the current ideal figure, such as liposuction, tucks, rib removal, cosmetic surgery. Over one million American women have had breast enlargement operations creating a $300-million business for plastic surgeons. Aren't there more important things to spend money on than the illusion of perfection?

We come in all sizes, all shapes, all colors—and we are all okay. Any cultural model is bound to be damaging and unhealthy if it becomes a requirement. Your body is not an object—it's *you*. Accept your body. Love yourself just the way you are. If you want to make some changes, you will be more successful by being respectful of and encouraging to yourself than by being rejecting and disgusted. Remember, *it's more important to be healthy than to be perfect*. If you care for yourself and enjoy living in your body, it will become your passport, not your prison. Your body has much to teach you; you can't have high self-esteem unless you love all of yourself—and that *includes* your beautiful thunder thighs!

Avoidance

Everyone has pain and discomfort at times. What do we learn to do with it?[5]

- **Deny.** On our honeymoon, my husband and I agreed that, unlike other couples, *we* wouldn't have problems. This set us up for a relationship based on denial and gunnysacking.

- **Distract.** Occasionally a movie or a change of scenery can provide a needed break. Too many romance novels or soap operas, however, can be an addiction, an escape from life.
- **Drug.** At home with three small children all day, a late afternoon glass of wine helped me survive the fatigue and calm the stress of the end of the day. On the other hand, this ritual kept me from confronting and dealing with my problems for a long time.

Everyone uses strategies of avoidance at times. They can provide a brief vacation—a time for regrouping or a change of perspective. The danger lies in using these strategies as a matter of course—when denial, distraction, and drugs become a way of life; a way to avoid dealing with life. When we avoid, we do nothing and nothing changes, except, perhaps, our perceptions.

We live in a drug culture. Drugs that didn't exist a decade ago are now permanent crutches to those who have no better solutions to their troubles. While warring against crack, we have as great a national addiction to legal drugs. For years, physicians have casually prescribed tranquilizers for unhappy people, instead of encouraging them to make changes in their lives. In 1960, Valium did not exist; now six billion tablets are consumed annually. The alcohol and tobacco industries spend millions on advertising, bombarding us with images of happiness through the consumption of addictive substances.

It takes more energy to avoid pain than to face it. When we avoid pain, we hold on to it. It becomes chronic. As long as we keep avoiding, we remain stuck in feelings of helplessness and numbness. We cut ourselves off from the compassion of understanding friends—and interrupt the process of healing. Sharing pain with others—as witnessed in funerals—allows an opening for giving and receiving support and for bonding.

Unhappy people and families don't become happy by pretending, denying, or avoiding reality. They become happy by talking, listening, negotiating, and making positive changes. They let go of self-defeating behavior that does not work.

In order for things to change, we must *do* something. We must attend to a flat tire—it does not fix itself. In figuring out how to solve a problem, we *do* something, we *change* something, and we *learn* something. When the problem is resolved, the pain is gone, and we are moving again. We are stronger and feel the joy of overcoming. We were put on this earth not to struggle, but to grow.

Alcohol Abuse

Children of alcoholics are at the highest risk for physical, sexual, and emotional abuse, for neglect, and for other forms of violence and exploitation. In about 90 percent of child-abuse cases, alcohol is a significant factor. When parents are drunk or "high," they often do things they later regret. Alcoholism and other drug addictions devastate families. In addition to physical damage, children of alcoholics experience a wide range of psychological difficulties, including learning disabilities, eating disorders, compulsive achieving, depression, shame, and guilt.

Adult children of alcoholics often have great difficulty with guilt, shame, control, trust, denial of feelings, and intimacy. They are far more likely to become alcoholics or marry one, and to suffer from relationship problems. Everyone's self-esteem and mental health is damaged.

An estimated 28 million Americans are children of alcoholics. They learn certain attitudes and behavior to survive. First and foremost, they learn to deny the problem. They also learn the rules: Don't talk. Don't trust. Don't feel. Those very skills that helped kids to survive at home later prevent them from thriving in life—from having healthy adult relationships. A friend's mother had another approach. She talked to her children about their alcoholic father; "Your dad's a good man, but he's sick."

Self-help groups are forming around the country for Adult Children of Alcoholics. ACA groups—along with AA groups, Al-anon, and Ala-Teen—can help participants to better understand the dynamics of alcoholic family systems. They can help a person learn to become a loving parent to their own wounded inner child. They can help to deal with alcoholism, and in the process of healing, prevent the disease from recurring in the next generation.

One ACA member in my workshop said, "Joining Adult Children of Alcoholics meetings has been the single most helpful and supportive thing I've done in my adult life. For the first time I understand why, for the past thirty-six years, I haven't felt good about myself, why I'm a caretaker and a perfectionist. It's such a relief to be in a room full of people who accept me as I am, who understand from the inside out what it's like, and to realize that I'm not bad, crazy, or sick—and that it's not hopeless. I've learned that it's okay to take care of myself and to like myself."

If your parents were alcoholic, it's not your fault. *You are not to blame.* You are not responsible for their problems. On the other hand, they may be responsible for some of yours. But *you* are responsible for the solution! Sort out in your mind what is yours and what is theirs.

Alcoholism is a family disease. *You hurt the worst those whom you love the most.* If addiction to alcohol or drugs runs in your family, break through the denial and deal with it—for your own sake and for the sake of your children.

Dualistic Thinking

In this society, we have a tendency to see things in terms of opposites—black and white, rich and poor, heaven and hell, day and night. This wouldn't be so bad if we didn't also put value judgments on such pairs, labeling some things "good" and other things "bad." Because we think this way, we have to be careful of the language we use with our children.

Did you ever do something stupid? Of course. We all have. But does that mean that you *are* stupid? Of course not! *What you do is not who you are.*

Remember a time when, as a child, someone pointed a finger at you and yelled, "You're a bad boy" or "You're a bad girl." What did you feel? Did you feel it again just now? How old were you at the time? One woman stated, "I did a dumb little thing, and with those words my mother wiped me out. Yelling that I was a 'bad girl' devastated me. I felt rejected, worthless, awful, and unlovable. Looking back, I realize that I wasn't a bad girl; I was a good girl who had made a dumb mistake."

Labels such as "bad," "clumsy," and "stupid" can be more powerful than they are meant to be. Value judgments applied to a person can damage self-esteem for years to come. Adults who give bad-kid messages probably do not understand the importance of separating the person from the behavior. In dealing with the unacceptable behavior, they reject the whole child, who feels wounded, shamed, worthless, and devastated.

It is possible to deal with unacceptable behavior without damaging anyone. *We must separate the person from the behavior.* Think about when you were a child. What was considered bad in your family? When did your parents and siblings use the word? In what context? After all your life experiences, what do you now consider to be bad? What do you want your children to think is bad?

Parents apply that word to many diverse behaviors, such as being noisy, forgetting a chore, getting a low grade, preferring a certain hairstyle. But instead of labeling the behavior bad; they label the whole child bad, which is certainly unfair. The child is inherently a good person who was, perhaps, just being forgetful, confused, or exercising poor judgment. Instead of getting a heavy dose of rejection, punishment, or shame, he or she needs understanding more than anything else.

When dealing with unacceptable behavior, do it privately. Treat children with respect and caring. Sit down with them; touch them supportively. *Love the doer, even when you don't like the deed.* Talk about what happened. Imagine that you can hang the problem behavior on the wall so that both can separate from it and discuss it objectively. What happened? What was the child thinking? What is he or she feeling? What did he or she learn? How can the situation be fixed? With this strategy you can both begin to see the gray area between good and bad, and the problem can get resolved without the child feeling rejected.

When children are labeled bad, they feel bad and behave badly—a self-fulfilling prophecy. They are good kids who may, at times, make mistakes or do dumb things, just as you once did. Don't label them anything but good, because they tend to believe you and become what you say they are. Believe that they are good. Expect them to be *good*—not *perfect*. Encourage and appreciate the behavior you want.

Comparison

"There were four girls in our family," a workshop participant told me. "We were always compared to each other in looks, intelligence, athletic ability, and so on. For the most part, I tried to hold my own by competing with my sisters. My youngest sister felt defeated and reacted by not participating at all. Most of my self-esteem problems stem from the fact that I was never as 'wonderful' as my oldest sister." Comparison is a setup for low self-esteem. Did your parents compare you with your siblings? Did they play favorites? How did you feel when they did that? What were they trying to do? Did it work? What is your present relationship with your siblings: Are you still competing?

Comparison makes our self-esteem dependent on competition, which is a win-lose game. If my success depends on your failure, then you will hope that I fail. Competition in everyday family life leads to anxiety, loss of self-confidence, and damaged trust. Comparison interferes with cooperation and teamwork. No one really wins.

Competitiveness has been considered a national virtue that brings out the best in us. Perhaps this is true—on the sports field. But in personal arenas, competition can make people suspicious and hostile toward others. Competition in school prompts children to stop trying in order to prevent failure. Competitors are less apt to trust or communicate with one another; they see themselves as separate, with conflicting goals. When we compete with and compare ourselves to others, We end up feeling like a failure because there's always someone better than me in one area or another: she's got a better figure, he has a way with words, she makes more money, and so on. All these thoughts can make us forget our own special gifts and qualities. Comparing ourseves with others is not an accurate measure of our inherent self-worth.

Often we trap ourselves by identifying the best qualities of many different people, synthesizing them into a fantasy ideal, and then trying—as a single human being—to live up to that impossible image. We put others on a pedestal while putting ourselves down, and our self-esteem suffers in the process. If we put ourselves up and others down, we create separation. We may feel smug or we may feel guilty; either way gets us nowhere.

We drive wedges between ourselves and other people by trying to be better than them—rather than enhancing our relationships by accepting our differences and doing our best for our own sakes. Likewise, when we base our own judgment and behavior on someone else's values, we separate ourselves from our own truths. My daughter describes this phenomenon as "compara-sin"; it's a sin to give away so much of our power.

We can let go of the tendency to compete. We can let go of the win-lose struggle. We can learn instead to be sincerely happy for others' achievements and successes. As one woman stated, "Edna's a good cook, so let her cook. I'm a good eater!" This shift from win-lose to win-win thinking makes life less stressful and more fun. A win-win attitude fosters the cooperation essential for having a winning family team.

Cooperation is necessary for healthy families and also for success in business. Working and pulling together is the solid foundation on which successful businesses and winning families alike are built.

Comparison encourages and enforces conformity. But no one has to be like everyone else! As a matter of fact, you *can't* be like everyone else, because you are one of a kind. It's okay to be who you really are. If you aren't you, who will be? Judy Garland used to tell her daughter, Liza Minelli, "Always be a first-rate version of yourself instead of being a second-rate version of someone else."

Since the beginning of time, billions of people have inhabited our planet. Yet there has never been anyone like you. You are unique. You are special. Your personality plus your experiences make you a divine original. The only person you can compare yourself with is you.

How are you today, compared with three months ago or three years ago? Are you more loving, more accepting? Are you a better person or are you backsliding? Compare yourself only with you and your own personal growth. Compete only with yourself. Challenge yourself to become your own personal best.

If you notice that you are comparing yourself to (and competing with) another person, change your self-talk. Instead of putting yourself down, consider the other person a model and lift yourself up. Even our children can be models. (I once observed my daughter on stage moderating a junior high school program; I told myself that if she could do it, so could I. Now, mysteriously, I have become a professional speaker!) We are hungry for models. Seeing with new eyes, we can find people everywhere who can inspire us to excellence. When we change our thinking from "you or me" to "you and me," we enjoy ourselves and each other far more. We can feel a connection with rather than a separation from others.

Seeing People as Objects

There are two ways of viewing people. In an I-thou relationship, we can accept people as themselves and see them as they really are, but in an I-it relationship, we objectify them. Objectification of others—that is, seeing people as objects—has a natural use and value, as it helps us to organize the world. But it also forms the roots for racism and sexism, along with personal alienation in our families and in society.

Seeing the world in terms of external or surface characteristics—nationality, race, sex roles, disabilites—helps children simplify and organize a complex world. But the categories—the stereotypes—become filled with hand-me-down beliefs, fears, and other emotional baggage that create distance, distrust, and disrespect. When people *look* for differences, that's all they see.

When I was young, my German family was the target of suspicion and prejudice during World War II. My Uncle Franz, a quiet barber who spoke imperfect English, was suspected of being a Nazi. Since Hitler's army was the most horrifying expression of racism we had ever known, the fear was understandable. Yet being associated with that stereotype was a threat to the entire family and frightened us all. Similarly, in California, thousands of Japanese-Americans were rounded up and placed in concentration camps. Those victims of prejudice and fear suffered because they were seen as objects.

Growing up, we have all learned stereotypes: that it is not okay to be red, black, brown, or yellow, Jewish, disabled, gay, or female (or more recently, some say, white and male). We have all suffered from prejudice. Prejudice is often subtle; but discrimination is evident in education and employment, and in social status. The results are victimization, poverty, and low self-esteem in entire groups of people. When we internalize prejudice and social rejection, we can perpetuate our attitudes and turn on ourselves and others like us. An alternative is to name the source of the problem. Black parents can correctly teach their children that there is nothing wrong with them, only with the way the world treats them. This is a perfect example of how building self-esteem can change the world.

Millions of people who fall into "minority" categories are ignored or treated like objects. They are not taken seriously. Negative judgments are based on comparison to an "ideal" image of how these groups are supposed to be—according to stereotyped roles. These images often lie outside of our awareness until they are challenged in some way and brought to our consciousness.

There are also many gender stereotypes in our culture that interfere with communication. Macho men and seductive women are two of the most obvious; if couples play these games with one another, though, they will never learn to trust one another. This is why pornography is so dangerous. It reinforces the images telling us that sex is loveless, that women and children like to be hurt, and that treating people as objects is acceptable and normal. These ideas are not true, and in fact are far from normal. (Molesters of over 87 percent of girls and 77 percent of boys admitted to imitating behavior in pornographic publications.) The porn industry sets up women and young children as objects of "pleasure" to be used and abused, and frighteningly enough, the largest consumers of pornography are impressionable children from 12 to 17 years of age.

Objectification dehumanizes people by stripping them of their individuality, their *person*ality, and justifies treating them as worse than machines. It is easy to be violent toward objects since objects don't have feelings. Our built-in prejudices cause us all to suffer, because they keep us from seeing clearly. It's not a question of whether we are prejudiced, but how. If we can begin by acknowledging it in ourselves, we can take steps toward changes.

We live in a culturally diverse society, where all people are created equal. Instead of putting ourselves and others down, we need to lift ourselves and others up. Instead of identifying with the lowest common denominators, we need to see the specialness in every human being. We need to see strengths in differences, not weaknesses or threats.

No matter what your race, ethnic origin, sex, or sexual preference, you are OKAY! You are a subject, not an object; you are you. To counter and heal destructive prejudice, affirm your own worth and that of others; black is beautiful—and white, yellow, and red are, too. We have to rid ourselves of our mental shackles and join with our brothers and sisters for support, for healing, and for strengthening our pluralistic society.

For high self-esteem we need acceptance. It's crucial that we give it to ourselves and to others. Remember the Golden Rule: "Do unto others as you would have done unto you!"

Seeing Ourselves as Objects

Unfortunately, what we would have done unto ourselves is sometimes less than respectful. Objectification of others— whether in a positive or negative light—teaches us to objectify ourselves. If I have a picture in my head of how the "ideal you" is supposed to behave in an "ideal relationship," this means that an "ideal me" must play a certain role as well. When we expect ourselves to fit such images, the roles we play cut us off from any other reality—like who we really are. We acknowledge behavior that is consistent with our image, and filter out any information that doesn't fit. Therefore, we can share only certain parts of ourselves with others—and with ourselves. Controlling the world to fit my illusions, I can never honestly get to know myself—

or you. I won't be able to know or truly love you if you grow out of my ideal of you.

Objectifying ourselves leads to performance ("Smile for the camera!"), second-guessing, pretense, stress, and a lopsided focus on externals. We can spend a lifetime doing what we imagine others want us to do—only to find out that they never wanted us to do that at all. A friend of mine and her husband moved to a new state. There, dissatisfied with their new house and location, they discovered that neither of them had actually wanted to move—but did it because each thought the other did! We can waste our lives never doing what we want, or not even knowing what we want, because we're caught up in an imaginary structure that has little to do with reality.

Our images cause us a lot of trouble. Marriages hit the rocks when she realizes that "Mr. Right" can't be three places at once, or when the "perfect wife" suddenly loses her enthusiasm for keeping the "dream house" clean. How do healthy young parents respond when the apple of their eye is diagnosed with muscular dystrophy—or becomes handicapped in another way? What do upstanding, respectable parents do when their track star son announces he's gay? Or when "daddy's little girl" becomes pregnant as a teenager? What happens when the image is shattered? What do we do when it's not happening the way it's "supposed to"?

Such crises force us to make a choice: between the image we have in our heads and the real person in our lives, who is changing and growing—and who challenges us also to grow. Here's where we must face the alternative to "I-it" objectification, and create an "I-thou" relationship. This shift challenges us to let go of rigid expectations and stereotypes that are too high, too low, or in conflict with the individual. The shift calls us to look deep into the other person, seeing his or her capability rather than disability, looking beyond the differences to the commonality.

In the "I-thou" approach, images and expectations of how people are supposed to be are put aside or suspended. We open our minds, instead, to see that person right now, without labels, without the distortion of past memories. We can see how they are changing. Instead of filtering out—denying—everything that doesn't fit our image, we are open and willing to let in new experiences and information. Instead of being judgmental, we can be compassionate.

This "I-thou" relationship applies not only to our kids and spouses, but also to friends and strangers—and to ourselves. Instead of going through the motions of playing out our roles automatically, we can take a breath and make the shift to allow the inner process to happen.

It's okay to be who you really are. In fact, it's important, as a parent, that you are first and foremost a real person. Then look at your kids, beneath the externals. See beyond their appearance, their performance, and their behaviors. See the beauty and richness that make them unique and lovable.

It's a relief to realize that you don't always have to be perfect for other people. You don't always have to be on top of things; you don't always have to be strong. You're human—with good and bad days. That's okay. When you accept your humanness (even the yucky parts), your kids will more readily accept theirs— and will show you their true, brilliant colors.

Making this shift brings excitement and aliveness; it presents a constantly changing and expanding world. It may also bring some discomfort as the old objectifying, dehumanizing ways thaw out and the "real world"—of emotions, insecurity, and exhilaration—rushes in. Communication is no longer guarded but is open to learning about yourself and others. This increases honesty and integrity, freedom, meaningful friendships, and personal growth.

It is important to be aware of our own thoughts and feelings. And it is equally important to be willing to let them go in order to be open to the exciting process of being human—understanding, appreciating, and enjoying growth and change. Winning families are made up of people who constantly work to see themselves and others as dynamic, worthwhile persons, not trapping others as objects of the roles they play.

The Win-Lose System

Nobody likes to lose, yet mostly we're made to feel like losers. Often, focusing on faults and failures, people talk themselves into becoming losers. The win-lose system, in which only one person wins and everyone else loses, is hard on self-esteem.

We need to expand our definition of winning. Every success, accomplishment, or achievement, every task crossed off a "to-do list" is a win! We are winning all the time. Often, however, our wins go unnoticed and unappreciated by ourselves and others—and our self-esteem sags.

Pause for a moment and make a list of ten wins of the last few days. They can be big or little achievements—for example, getting to work or school on time, asking for something you wanted, changing seventeen diapers without complaining, or fixing a nice dinner for the family last night. Now give yourself a big pat on the back. You deserve it because you are a winner. You deserve more appreciation. You can't appreciate something if you don't notice it. So start looking for the wins.

When you crawl into bed tonight, don't think of what you didn't finish, what you should have done, what you could have done better. Instead, look for the wins. Every night before you turn off the light, make a list of ten things you did well, and you'll sleep like a baby. The next day, you will wake up feeling refreshed and positive about your life.

Instead of hoping that someone will notice and appreciate you, *give that to yourself.* You know when you did a good job; tell yourself so. Give yourself a pat on the back. Appreciation for ourselves and others can turn duty into a gift. It makes us much healthier and more fun to be around. A "winning is everything" attitude in life and sports can devastate self-esteem.

Sports have a powerful, long-lasting impact on children's lives. Coaches, teachers, and parents—with good intentions—may cause humiliation and frustration, anger and anxiety, failure and rejection in kids which will last much longer than the game season. If children are treated with dignity, encouragement, and support, being on the team can foster a sense of belonging, self-confidence, and fun. How the game is played and coached is as important as winning.

Positive self-esteem is essential for mental health and happiness. It is a necessary ingredient of a winning family. Yet our culture is very hard on self-esteem, presenting many barriers to mental health and happiness. We do our best, based on the information we have. Frequently our knowledge is incomplete, or we are misinformed, or we believe in myths that simply do not apply to our lives. When what we know is incorrect, things don't work out. "I did everything I was supposed to" I once exclaimed. "Why do I feel so bad?"

Now that you are aware of some of the barriers to gaining and maintaining self-esteem, they can become merely stumbling blocks. You can seek out solid information, unlearn what doesn't work, and learn what does. Then you can pass on better information to your kids so they can have their feet on solid ground sooner than you did. Once we see clearly, we can help our children avoid the same pitfalls in their own lives. Once we identify the stumbling blocks, we can turn them into stepping stones for personal growth and higher self-esteem.

The questions
Which frighten and make us want to run,
Which evade our socialized minds,
Which have never before been asked—
These are the questions which
We must dare to pursue,
The edges we must explore.

21

Who's Pulling Your Strings?

"To be nobody but yourself in a world which is doing its best to make you just like everybody else means to fight the greatest battle there is or ever will be."[1]

e. e. cummings

For most of my life I did just what I was "supposed" to do. On a day-to-day basis, I automatically carried out the musts, have tos, and ought tos that had been running my life. Then I learned the twelfth commandment: "Thou shalt not should upon thyself."[2]

I started to listen to my self-talk. Surprised at the string of orders bossing me around, I tuned in more closely. When I heard, "You have to wash the kitchen floor," I looked over my shoulder, wondering who had said that. I sat myself down and had a little talk with myself. "Self," I asked, "do you choose to clean the kitchen floor?" "Well," my Self answered, "I can't walk barefoot any more. My feet stick to the floor." After this little discussion, I decided that I wanted to wash the floor so I could walk barefoot and enjoy it. Doing this chore, then, wasn't half bad, because I had chosen to do it! That was the beginning of the long, gradual process of learning to use my internal locus of control.

Growing up is the process of making the shift from an external to an internal authority, or locus of control. When children are little, they have an external locus of control. They look to their parents and other important adults for information, for values, for direction. Like little sponges, they absorb and accept everything in their environment—believing it—and they internalize it. As they develop and mature, they gradually learn to think for themselves, trust themselves, become themselves. They learn to stand on their own two feet. They gain in confidence and competence. Ideally, as parents empower them and let go of control, children assume more responsibility and control over their own lives.

For many people, however, this important developmental process has been interrupted or thwarted; many adults, who were not empowered by their parents, still trust others more than they trust themselves. They are overly concerned about what others might say, what others might think, and what might please or displease others. (You know you're in big trouble if you're afraid to touch the pillow tags that say "Do not remove under penalty of law!")

Many people trust others more than they trust themselves. They don't know their own values, opinions, beliefs, habits, or identity. They look outside of themselves for approval, for a sense of worth, for happiness. Fully grown adults, they may still look to others to clean up after themselves or to rescue them from problems.

People with an external locus of control tend to be extremely dependent on persons and things outside of themselves; they give their power away, then feel powerless and out of control. In neglecting their own values, desires, dreams, and intuition, they lack identity and individuality. These people are the ones who, if their physician tells them they have six months to live, die obediently right on schedule. Seeking solutions outside of themselves, they are vulnerable to manipulation and exploitation by others and can easily become addicted to unhealthy relationships, drugs, food, entertainment, work, and possessions.

Unfortunately, our Western consumer culture is much too concerned with external things. Our appearance, performance, achievements, and possessions are given tremendous importance. (Americans have 400 times more possessions now than in the 1940s!) The internal world—what we think, what we need, what we value, what gives us meaning in life—is often ignored or considered unimportant. Thus, we are encouraged to remain children—dependent on external displays of identity, external sources of self-worth. We yield our power to vague external authorities of fashion, fads, and status symbols.

If we look around, we notice that the most interesting, impressive, and expressive people we know are the ones who have, at some point, decided to take charge of their lives. The truly successful people are the ones who succeed on their own terms— by writing their own rules and becoming their own authority. Dr. Bernie Siegel, author of *Love, Medicine, and Miracles*, writes about his cancer patients who are exceptions to the rule that cancer is incurable.

> Exceptional patients manifest the will to live in its most potent form. They take charge of their lives even if they were never able to before, and they work hard to achieve health and peace of mind. They do not rely on doctors to take the initiative but rather use them as members of a team, demanding the utmost in technique, resourcefulness, concern, and openmindedness. If they're not satisfied, they change doctors.[3]

These people have tapped into their inner locus of control, and their lives will never be the same again because they have found this wisdom. But we do not have to go to the threshold of death to find it. We can give ourselves permission now.

Where is *your* locus of control? Do you do things more to please others or to please yourself? Do you listen more to the external voices—the musts, have tos, ought tos—or do you listen more to your secret internal voices—your intuition?

Begin to bring your locus of control inside yourself: Make a list of five things that you have to, ought to, or are supposed to do today. Start each sentence with "I." Then rewrite your list, beginning each sentence, instead, with "I choose to." Notice the difference you feel. Now you are in control. As an adult, you have power over your own life. You have created the life you now live and can make changes.

Turn off the television, the radio, and the walkman. Relax! Then listen. Turn down the endless bombardment of noise and chatter. Listen! Listen to your soft inner voices. Then do what is good for you. Quiet time can be the most important time in your life. Take long walks. Listen to your body. Learn to trust it. Meditate. Write in a journal.

In Western civilization we have learned to overvalue certain facets of ourselves and undervalue others. The rational and logical aspects are respected and developed, while the irrational—feelings and intuition—are dismissed, depreciated, and denied. Other civilizations, past and present, approach life with deep respect for and awareness of the intuitive element of our existence. Tune in to "inner listening"—the divine guidance system that "makes clearer to us what we really want, as distinct from what we have been talked into."[4] Learn to trust yourself. Use your own mind and body, feelings and intuition, and you're an autonomous adult—your own person.

When we raise a family, we begin with externally oriented little children who learn their value (and everything else) from the important people in their lives. In the process of helping them to grow up, we can move from controlling statements ("Do

as you're told") to empowering statements ("Think for yourself").
Parents can nudge their children toward becoming internally
motivated adults who think for themselves, who trust themselves,
and who have high self-esteem and personal power.

Here are suggestions to nurture the inner development of
your children.

- Develop and enjoy the bond of love between you and
  your kids.
- Accept them as they are (though not necessarily all of
  their behaviors). Give them permission to be individuals.
  Provide understanding, support, and nurturing.
- Accept and understand their needs and feelings. Your
  children are unique beings with their own ideas and
  desires.
- Honor their separateness from you. When possible, let
  them do things their own way. Give them permission to
  be individuals. Let them teach you.
- Encourage them to think for themselves, to make decisions and goals based on what they want and need, what
  they think is best. If "everybody's doing it," assist your
  kids in sorting out the situation and consequences, and
  help them decide what they feel is right.
- Listen to their experiences, stories, and opinions.
- Offer choices. (Would you rather have your birthday
  party at home or in the park this year?)
- Support and encourage healthy exploration of their
  world, while setting reasonable and healthy limits.
- Use assertive communication instead of games, force,
  and manipulation.
- Use the natural-and-logical-consequences style of discipline. It teaches children to figure things out, to think
  for themselves, and to become self-disciplined.
- Use more encouragement and less praise. Praise is a

verbal reward that shows children that they are pleasing to others. Encouragement motivates them from within—from being pleased with themselves. They gain higher self-esteem directly from the experience.

- Give children a box of stars, so they can be in charge of rewarding themselves.
- Encourage your children to go after what they want. Goal setting in little things teaches them important skills they'll need later on in life.
- Give both boys and girls the same empowering messages. Girls have a greater tendency toward learned helplessness, which is detrimental to self-esteem and success later in life.
- Encourage your kids to take quiet time in the afternoon. They may complain of boredom at first. That's okay. A classmate once pointed out that the most creative and best times of her childhood came shortly after she announced that she was bored. She had to look inside herself for entertainment!

You can foster growth in your children as you cultivate it in yourself. As you get in touch with your own inner wisdom, you can trust that it will guide you in the fine art of parenting. Your family can become one of centered individuals, each leading interesting and healthy lives.

"Follow your bliss."[5]

Joseph Campbell

22

Play

"Joy is not in things; it is in us."[1]

Richard Wagner

I once attended a kazoo concert—a "Kazoophony." The musicians (who claimed to have attended the Eastman Kazoovatory of Music) played "The 1813 Overture" and "The Plight of the Kazoomblebee." The kazoo, they said, is to classical music what a total body cast is to ballet. Needless to say, it was not an evening of soaring and inspiring elegance, but those performers sure rediscovered silliness—and they are rewarded for it by bringing joy and laughter into people's lives.

Play is a universal language and one of the healthiest things in our culture. When we play, we give a gift of joy and spontaneity to one another. The thrill of being alive pervades our entire body when we play. Families—and life—are supposed to be fun.

"Take me into your world," I once told my children, "and show me what you see." Leaving my parent-self at home, we walked along the irrigation ditch to the bridge where the troll lives. We stopped along the narrow path in front of a crooked tree ("Put your feet right here, Mom, stoop down, and squint.") and showed me where to look to see the figure of a Dr. Seuss creature in the trunk. I had passed that way many times before, but I had never been able to see it before! This was my initiation into their magical, mystical, and wonder-filled world. That experience bridged the worlds of parent and child in which we each lived, separately, and that memory enriches me still.

Children are our natural teachers, but to learn best from them we must meet them at their level. They can help us remember how to play—how to break all the rules and write our own. A chair can be a fort or a fire engine; an adult can be the baby when the kids play "house." My children have encouraged me to try new games—like hackey-sack and riding a skateboard—and have helped me to remember some wonderful old ones like hide and seek and squirt-gun fights. Through our children, we can see the world with fresh eyes. With them we can cut loose from stuffy adultness, be totally foolish—and get away with being unforgivably silly! We can reclaim forgotten parts of ourselves and rediscover the finer points of childhood.

What did you love to do as a kid? Remember those adventures and tricky games? Share them with your kids! Have you shared your jacks and marbles with them? If kids don't learn to play when they are young, they may never learn.

To many kids with a high TV diet, play means passively waiting to be entertained. As a result, they don't learn to actively entertain themselves. Put-downs, humiliation, and violence are often the forms of "humor" we find on television; canned laughter marks the pauses where the watching audience is "supposed to" laugh. Kids learn from commercials that they can't play without the expensive games and toys that are in fashion at the time. They need encouragement to discover their own creativity through the excitement of building a dam or a treehouse from scratch.

When my daughter was in her teens, she once complained that to many people her age, "fun" meant watching TV or videos or drinking beer. If there was no free beer at a party, it was reason enough not to go. So they sat around feeding their addictions and wondering, "Are we having fun yet?"

Kids are born with inner joy. Play is as natural to them as breathing. For kids, there is no separation between work and play. Work is play until parents teach them that it's work—and only then do they learn to resist it. They quickly pick up the dualistic thinking of the adult world: Work is what you have to do and don't like, and play is what you love to do but don't have time for. Yet work can become play with an adult's attitude shift. Having a vegetable garden, for example, can either be drudgery, or sheer joy. If we put fun back into our own work, we will want to do it and our kids will be more eager to join in.

Childhood is a time of phenomenal growth, aliveness, and discovery. Growing up, for many, has meant ending this amazing process. A young man once said to me, "Growing up in America is the process of growing numb." Many have come to associate growing up with a loss of excitement and eagerness to learn. Playfulness has slowly disappeared from their lives. Yet this need not be a terminal condition. Ask a kid how to play and you can begin to recapture dormant parts of yourself, bringing aliveness, spontaneity, and joy back into your life.

When my kids were young, I collected rhythm instruments. Periodically we would turn on some lively music and all become percussionists. Sometimes we took out hats—or made them—to add to the fun, and marched and paraded around the house. (Rhythm toys are great for adult parties, too; we would make sure to give the cymbals to the most reserved person there!) We also acted out "Peter and the Wolf." I'd put on the record, and the living room would suddenly transform into a meadow, each of us playing a character and identifying with the instruments and themes. There was almost always an argument over who got which parts, but this charade was a wonderful way to spend an evening together. The children learned to appreciate classical music, as well.

If you aren't already playing with your kids, here are some
helpful tips.

- Play needs to be fun for everyone. When you tease or
  tickle your kids, watch them; if it's not fun for them,
  stop doing it. Some parents toss a baby into the air, saying "What fun!" and continue even if the baby starts to

cry. If you're both not having fun, change the game. Kids may feel violated by well-meaning parents and older siblings who tease them too far.

- Play is best when everyone comes out winning. If you really want your kids to win, you will coach and cheer for them and be happy when they succeed. "New Games" are noncompetitive games that involve everyone. Tail of the Dragon, for example, involves a line of people, each holding onto the waist of the person in front of them. A kerchief (the tail) hangs from the pocket of the last person, and the first person (the head) tries to catch it.[2]

- When parents feel they have to beat their kids at a game, the kids are set up to lose. This isn't play, but a power ploy with the losers being victimized. Parents are bigger, older, and smarter than kids; they can win all the time if they want to. Kids who lose all the time become discouraged and don't want to play anymore because they know they will lose. Nobody likes to lose. The parent may win the game, but the relationship suffers, as does the child's attitude toward play. If your parents played with you in this way, remember how it felt. Did you ever shrug and say, "It doesn't matter," when in fact it did? That kind of play wasn't fair—and it wasn't fun. Try a new kind of game with your kids, or at least let them win sometimes.

- Folk wisdom states, "A dirty kid is a happy kid." Telling your kid, "Go out and play but don't get dirty" is setting a double standard and can lead to disappointment on someone's part. Kids often do get dirty when they're having a good time. A dirty, excited kid is healthier than a clean, depressed one.

Playing will develop your sense of humor, along with that of your kids. A regular dose of giggles and snorts does wonderful, even astonishing, things for your emotional and physical health and well-being. A sense of humor can be a saving grace in times of stress, and a survival tool throughout life.

Norman Cousins, a one-time business executive, was told by his physicians that he had a chronic, debilitating disease. He refused to believe that he would only get worse, then die. He decided to do anything necessary to defeat the disease process. If we can create disease in our bodies by negative thoughts, beliefs, and attitudes, he reasoned, we also have the power to reverse that process and create healthy bodies instead.

Every day Cousins watched old Charlie Chaplin movies and laughed until his sides ached. He filled his hospital room with laughter and giggles. Over time he succeeded in reversing his "terminal" disease, and regained perfect health![3] So laugh often (there's always something to laugh at); it will make you healthy.

Not only does laughter stimulate the immune system, it relaxes you and raises your guard against depression and pain. Exercise is a form of play for many—running, dancing, hiking, swimming, and biking. And the people you play and laugh with easily become your friends. Play in a family increases health, happiness, and harmony. It creates bonds between people and enhances personal growth and self-esteem. A gift that keeps giving, your play of today builds a store of rich memories for you to draw on as time moves along.

Life is a burden to those who don't enjoy themselves. Other people are a burden to them, and they are even a burden to themselves. Enjoying ourselves, on the other hand, is one of the greatest things we can do for ourselves. And because joy is contagious, others will benefit, too.

Be silly at times. The word silly comes from ancient roots meaning "happy," "prosperous," or "blessed." It's good to be silly and to allow silliness in your kids. It's a sign of aliveness; depressed children are not silly. Record or remember the really funny words and events of childhood (your own and your children's), so that you can recycle the joy when you are all older.

Kids are a great excuse to be silly. Alone, you might not spontaneously roll down a grassy hill, lest someone think you berserk, but if you take a kid along, no one will think twice. If they do, it will probably be, "How wonderful to see parents playing with their children!"

Seek out and share natural highs with your family—adventures, art, making music, cuddling, laughter, excitement. Look for beautiful sunsets and rainbows. Share the amazement, the awe, with each other. Natural highs may be an important key to alcohol and drug-abuse prevention. When people are high on life, they don't need alcohol and drugs.

Sharing the wonder and beauty of nature has many benefits. It can build respect and allow for bonding with each other and with the earth. It can heal strained relationships. It can also give children a feeling of security—a sense that they are part of the grand plan.

One of our peak family experiences happened when my kids and I were at the edge of a small lake catching tadpoles. My youngest came to me with a closed fist and wide-open eyes. He placed an enormous pollywog with budding hind legs into my hand, and my face lit up also. I could feel the creature's heart beating! The magic and mystery of that moment still thrill me.

Start to play today. Look for things that tickle your funny bone. Put down this book and do one fun thing you love to do. Right now. You deserve joy in your life; it's never too late to have a happy childhood! Make fun time a high priority in your family. Set aside a half day to play together. Go for a walk or a bike ride. Go to the museum or the zoo. Be silly with your kids at least once a day.

Family playtime increases closeness and positive feelings. Everyone relaxes and feels more alive. Love just happens when you're having fun together. Tape this cliché on your refrigerator: *The family that plays together stays together!*

23

The Winning Environment

"If a seed is given good soil and plenty of water and sun,
it doesn't have to try to unfold.
It doesn't need self-confidence or self-discipline or perseverance.
It just unfolds. As a matter of fact, it can't help unfolding."[1]

Barbara Sher

Humans—and all forms of life—have basic needs. The need for sunshine, water, healthy food, and fresh air are fundamental to self-esteem. If they are not met, there is little chance of creating an environment that is nurturing to the soul. There is much reason for concern about our physical surroundings; their impact on our physical, mental and emotional health is subtle but vital. Raising healthy children is our most important work. Creating and sustaining a positive climate—a home in which they can survive and thrive—is essential to our task as parents.

Like plants, human beings need optimal growing conditions in order to thrive. When children are not raised with these conditions, their growth and development may be impaired. Seeds may lie dormant for a long time until the environment improves—the sun shines, the rain comes, a rock is moved away. Then these seeds can grow, blossom, and bear fruit.

Remembering your family environment as a child, consider the following questions.

- Could you trust your parents—knowing that they would take care of your needs (food, shelter, acceptance, and love) and protect you from harm?
- Were you respected and loved just for being you?
- Did your parents realize that you were unique and special, and make you feel that way?
- Did they believe in you and encourage you to be your best?
- Did you feel that your ideas and opinions were taken seriously?
- Were you encouraged to discover and explore your special talents and interests?
- Did they encourage you to do things for yourself—including solving your own problems?
- Did they both set limits and allow freedom?
- Were you told that you could be and do anything you wanted? Were you given support and encouragement to do so?
- Did you know that when you got in over your head you could turn to them for help—without reproach?[2]

If you answered yes to many of these questions, yours was probably a winning environment. If you answered no to many of them, you must realize that you have had some obstacles to achieving high self-esteem. Your parents probably gave you more than they received. They probably did the best they could at parenting, which is the most difficult and challenging job of all. Your parents made mistakes, as we all do; learn from them and forgive them. Be grateful for all the good things they gave you.

We are all winners. But some people disguise themselves as losers. In their childhood environment, perhaps no one saw their beauty or made them feel beautiful. Perhaps no one saw their hidden greatness and the important gifts they had for the world. Perhaps no one believed in them, supported them, or encouraged them to become winners. They became losers because they had no idea that they really were winners.

Many people who lacked important emotional nutrients as children become late bloomers. They fill their areas of deficiency and learn new skills. They grow, blossom, and bear fruit. It is never too late to become the beautiful, healthy, and happy person you were meant to be.

Imagine how different your life would be now if you had grown up in a winning environment. Imagine what your family of today might become if you were to create a winning environment. All children have the potential for becoming winners. If they can be winners in their own families, they are on the road to a successful life.

It all begins with a decision. You can use all the tools in this book—affirming yourself and your children, finding new ways to talk and play together You can make big changes a little at a time. You cannot turn back the clock, but you can begin to change now.

As you create a healthier environment for your children, you create it for yourself. As you create it for yourself, you create it for your children. At first it may be hard work—change is usually difficult. But it will get easier and better. Be patient. It takes time. Each little change is a movement toward becoming a Winning Family.

24

Extending Your Family

"The bond that links your true family is not one of blood, but of respect and joy in each other's life."[1]

Richard Bach

Before America became urbanized earlier this century, most American families were multigenerational, extended families. They were not only the center of work, education, recreation, and worship; they also constituted economic production units. In rural settings, cooperation was necessary for survival.

Kids would see how grandparents, aunts, and uncles got along with others, how they made judgments and decisions, how they solved problems. They would learn about life from various people they trusted. They watched adults handle important human emotions and major life events: marriage, childbirth, sickness, and death. If a parent died, other relatives would fill in to keep the family going.

Rubbing elbows with lots of relatives, children learned to get along with different types of people. Many adults shared responsibility for the children. Working side by side with others, children got direct on-the-job training for living.

I grew up in an extended family in Detroit. My Germanimmigrant parents met there and married shortly afterward. My father's brother, Franz, lived with the family for twenty years. Uncle Franz was a barber. As a child, I would sit on his lap and comb his hair. I would walk with him to visit his friends. I saw his world and how he related to it. I learned much from him. Sharing special time together, we developed a loving bond between us. His presence in my family was a key to my self-esteem.

Families have changed dramatically—from the extended family, to the nuclear family, and now to an amazing diversity of family forms. Children of today grow up in a variety of family units. One in five children lives in a "blended" or stepfamily. One in four lives in a single-parent family. More than half the children under age six are cared for by a childcare provider while parents work. And there are millions of "latchkey" children who are home alone after school until a parent comes home from work.

Today we have smaller households; a greater proportion have few or no children, and there are an increasing number of single-person households. Individuals are more isolated, more alone. A man I know commented that when he was growing up, neighbors would always poke their heads through the kitchen door in the morning and ask, "Is the coffee on?" Where he lives today, he is on speaking terms with his neighbors, but only to the point of making small talk about the car or the weather. The days of neighborhoods serving as community support groups are all but gone.

Every year in the United States, forty million people move from one place to another.[2] They uproot themselves for a variety of reasons; many move great distances, leaving grandparents, friends, and neighbors behind. Some move to withdraw from the pain and problems of dysfunctional families. Some move to pursue job or educational opportunities. Transplanting their families to new settings, they must start over from the beginning— re-creating important connections with others.

Within the last fifty years there have been enormous splits in families—physically and emotionally; the two often go hand in hand. For many, important natural family connections have been seriously weakened or severed. At the same time, we are also seeing a rise in the numbers of immune system-related illnesses such as AIDS, Chronic Fatigue Syndrome, Epstein-Barr virus, and lupus. A strong and flexible family and social network is a metaphor for the body's natural ability to maintain its resistance to disease.

In the case of divorce, the vital grandparent-grandchild bond is frequently interrupted or damaged at a time when kids most desperately need support and stability. In the past, aunts and uncles and grandparents often filled in during times of crisis until the family recovered. Kids had someone familiar to cling to throughout the turmoil. Divorce stems from problems between husband and wife. It need not create a major rift between two families. The kids are not divorcing a parent, or grandparents, aunts, or uncles for that matter. Noncustodial parents can continue to have a tremendous influence in the life and self-esteem of their children. It's important to maintain a strong, loving bond. Give them time (high-quality visits) and attention (letters and phone calls), and be sensitive to their needs. The human connection is more important than the role played within a family system.

It is possible for divorced couples to heal their wounds over time and even to become friends with each other. In this new style of extended family, there is less pain and harm to the kids and the rest of the family. I have a friend who is on such good terms with her ex-husband (and his second wife) that she is godmother to their two children, and although they live over a thousand miles apart, they see each other at least once a year.

Mothers-in-law have inherited an unfortunate cultural stereotype. Unfairly labeled "the enemy," they are the butt of many jokes that set them up for rejection, divisiveness, and pain. The same is true for stepmothers. Although it is difficult to blend two families, negative stereotypes can undermine the quality of the grandparent-grandchild, stepparent-stepchild connection.

Grandparents are natural self-esteem developers, who give us a long-range perspective on life and are a great source of information on our personal family history, yet they often live too far away to maintain close contact with their grandchildren. These greatest of natural resources for making kids feel important may themselves be feeling unimportant, lonely, and unneeded hundreds of miles away. This loving cross-generational kinship connection has been dangerously weakened by modern day lifestyles. Yet it need not be this way.

Helen, a seventy-six-year-old grandmother who attended a workshop, works in a nursery school. After her own six children were grown, she got involved working with other people's kids. She loves doing it, and knows she's needed. The children are enriched with her loving presence, her depth of experience, and her wisdom. Kids in nursery schools and daycare centers everywhere would benefit from the involvement of loving elders.

Everyone needs someone to turn to when things get tough. The hard work of childrearing is lightened by having someone share laughter, a meal, a walk in the park. "Joy shared is joy doubled; sorrow shared is half sorrow." Studies show that a strong social support network is key to high self-esteem for children and parents alike. In a social context we learn more about ourselves and others. We learn to open up to life and involve ourselves in it. Friends encourage us to grow into ourselves, and accept ourselves for who we are.

When my children were young, a sixteen-year-old boy from Mississippi lived with our nuclear family for a summer. Paul did yard work for us and at times helped with the kids. We all enjoyed our "extended family" so much that we invited him back the following year. Today, despite the miles that separate us, a loving bond connects us; Paul is part of our family.

Later on, my daughter extended the family even further.

Attending college in Santa Fe, she interviewed with a family looking for a babysitter for their three young sons. It was love at first
sight, and gradually Kristen became part of their family, just as
Paul had become part of ours. When we visited her for the holidays, we were graciously, lovingly, and openly taken in by her
adopted family.

New varieties of extended families are becoming more widespread today. Consciously or unconsciously, people are seeking
out others to fill the void created by the absence of family members. Coworkers may become siblings or cousins. Neighbors may
fill in as aunts, uncles, or grandparents. Many families are sharing
their kids, spreading the responsibility around a bit, creating the
support they need, and enriching their lives.

People who have ongoing significant contact with children
—childcare providers, babysitters, neighbors—are part of an extended family. They play important roles in children's lives and
development. As kids get older, they may seek out and "adopt"
surrogate family members who can enrich their lives as well as
our own.

After creating a "surrogate family," Kathy (a workshop participant) reflected, "Our biological families contain structured
roles that lock us into a track of behavior much like a rollercoaster.
As we grow and change, it becomes difficult to break away from
these predefined roles. The surrogate family, by contrast, begins
at the point at which we leave the biological one. There are few
preconceived notions about each other, and we're allowed to be
ourselves. We can interact without the fear of criticism or comparison. We can choose our surrogate family members."

Parents can be each other's biggest supports. Another participant, Nancy, told me, "I have a friend whose husband works
nights, as does mine. We have two children each. One night a
week I have her kids over for dinner and to spend the night, and
the next week she takes mine. This gives the kids some quality
playtime and gives us a night off to spend some quality time

alone." This time together also builds connections between all four children that enhances their lives as well.

Many couples, with or without children, are choosing to have another person share their homes with them, creating the potential at least for developing deep bonds. These roommates live together through thick and thin, and often become part of each other's lives—even after they have separated.

In 1936, a group of twelve young mothers from a farm community in Colorado formed a social club called The Diligent Dozen so that they could go somewhere with their children and completely enjoy themselves. They had all moved West with their husbands, and met monthly to do mending and fancywork while their children played. Afterward they enjoyed games planned by the hostess. The husbands, who affectionately called the club The Dirty Dozen, were welcome if they came. They had big feasts at holidays. As the years went by and original members passed away, they invited new women to join. Through repeated contact, they developed a deep bond—"like family"—among themselves.[3]

The Mexican-American culture actively adds new members to "la familia." The best man and maid of honor at weddings and sponsors in baptism and confirmation ceremonies become "padrinos" and a part of the family. These multi-generational families keep expanding their connections.

We need many caring people in our lives. We need to reweave the web that connects us, so that we have a safety net when we slip. We need to come together in ways that matter, that sustain and enrich us. When we extend our families, we expand our lives.

25

The Winning Family

"The greatest gifts you can give your children are the roots
of responsibility and the wings of independence."[1]

Denis Waitly

Winning families come in a variety of forms, sizes, and colors.
They have qualities in common that contribute to a high level
of self-worth in their members. The climate is comfortable; people feel "at home" in their homes.

There is a strong sense of sharing and connectedness in a
family team Members know that they are important, that they
belong. Given the wings of independence, they are encouraged
to find and create their own meaning and purpose in life and to
realize their own dreams. Balancing closeness and separateness,
they enjoy spending time together as well as apart. Individuals
"do their own thing" and are also committed to the well-being
of the whole family.

One spring, my sons created a memorable winning event
My older son Damian offered to be the chauffeur for younger
Felix's senior prom. He borrowed a Mercedes-Benz from a pro-
fessor, decorated the inside with silk roses, and dressed for the
part. Being short on money, Felix and his friend Jeff decided to

cook dinner at our home. I ironed my best tablecloth and borrowed a silver candelabra and serving pieces.

The boys spent many hours shopping and cooking. Suddenly it was time to put on their tuxedos and leave. Damian chauffeured Felix to pick up his date, while I picked up the pieces in the kitchen. Later, exchanging cap for apron, the chauffeur became the waiter. He served the lobster tails, presenting them as "giant roly-polies."[2] Felix snapped his fingers nonchalantly and called for the "wine" (sparkling cider). With a flourish, Damian opened the wired-on champagne cap and uncovered a screw-on cap, which everyone sniffed without cracking a smile. Observing from the kitchen, I loved every minute of it!

The winning family operates on the principle that everyone has a right to come out on top. This team encourages and supports all its players in discovering their unique interests and talents. Through believing in, coaching, and helping one another, they set themselves up for success. No one has to lose. "If I help you meet your goals, I win; if you help me reach mine, you win." The underlying belief is that everyone can come out winning. No one, therefore, has a desire to win at another's expense.

To create a winning family, it is necessary to redefine winning. Winning can no longer be defined as competing with, overpowering, intimidating, and putting others down. That is the win-lose model. A new definition of winning is to be your best and do the best you can. A desire for excellence—in oneself and for others—is the trait of a real winner.

Winning families are made up of high-quality relationships based on mutual respect, acceptance, honesty, trust, cooperation, loyalty, and faith in others. The parents honestly know and accept themselves, including their feelings and weaknesses. They can therefore accept feelings and weaknesses in each other and in their children. The win-win belief is relational; one can't be a winner without caring, sharing, and empowering others to win.

The well-being of individuals is a high priority. Rules—as

few as possible and as many as necessary—are made for the benefit of the whole family, not just the rulemaker. Rules validate and promote self-worth in individuals and harmony in the family. Parents create rules on the basis that human life and feelings are more important than anything else.

In winning families, people are listened to and heard. They enjoy spending time with each other. Everything is out in the open; there is no need for secrets or dishonesty. Family members are genuine with each other; they don't have to pretend or play a role. They know they are accepted and loved for who they are.

This healthy family has an openness to new people and new ideas. The whole family system is adaptable to life's changes—including new role definitions—and accepts and encourages change as a potential source of growth.

The climate is characterized by aliveness, genuineness, and love. It is okay to take risks. It is safe to be honest and real. A winning family is a high self-esteem team.

The "perfect family" model that is held up to us as an ideal never has problems. Everyone is always happy, always smiling, always clean. Expectations of perfection—to be a perfect parent, a perfect husband or wife, a perfect kid—are setups for frustration, disappointment, anger, pretense, and low self-esteem. The perfect family is a myth. It is a performance—like posing for a snapshot—that is a barrier to intimacy. It creates a great deal of stress when confused with real life.

On the other hand, the winning family is like a moving picture in which things are always happening, where people are changing and growing. A winning family is always in process. All families have problems, but members have skills to deal with them, and confidence that they will overcome them. When they need help, they have the wisdom to get it.

You can help to create a winning family—a family in which everyone feels like a success. It's worth the effort. Such great joy and depth of connection can happen by replacing old negative habits with new high self-esteem behaviors and attitudes. It all begins with a decision.

A winning family begins with parents who have a high level of self worth—the higher their own self-esteem and sense of competence, the more likely they are to create a winning family team. The winning family has nothing to do with awards or trophies. It has to do with liking, loving, and enjoying each other. It has to do with satisfaction. A winning family feels good.

26

A Winning World

"When we try to pick out anything by itself,
we find it hitched to everything else in the universe."[1]

John Muir

Before I had my first child, I never really looked forward in anticipation to the future. As I watched my son grow and learn, I began to imagine the world this generation of children would live in. I thought of the children they would have, and of their children. I felt connected to life both before my time and beyond it. Children are our link to future generations that we will never know.

"We did not inherit this land from our fathers.
We are borrowing it from our children."

Amish saying

I remember the first Earth Day back in April 1970; my young children proudly filled several bags with the trash that had littered a picnic area. When they were a little older, we all marched on the state capital to protest the Vietnam War. I've since watched my children grow into adults who believe in peace—and have the skills and the courage to create it in their own lives. I believe that my great-grandchildren will live in a better world for it.

As parents, we give our children the gift of life and the necessary tools to live it well. We need to love them completely and protect them from harm. Let us accept our responsibility and the challenge to make the world a truly safe and healthy environment for ourselves, for our loved ones, and for others. Let us be advocates for "all our relations," as the native peoples say—to improve the quality of life for all families.

We can extend our family to embrace people of different colors and lifestyles, people who speak different languages, people who come from and live in other lands. We are mysteriously interconnected with people around the globe. We are all related. We breathe the same air.

All families everywhere are supported and sustained by Mother Earth. We have a sacred connection with the planet that we cannot take for granted. Let us learn to walk lightly on the earth and to respect her as deeply as we do ourselves and our children.

We need to look at our beliefs about life on earth. If we say, "The problems we face are so immense, whatever we do doesn't matter," we overwhelm ourselves. We talk ourselves into being helpless and hopeless. If, instead, we tell ourselves that we must learn to live in harmony with each other for the sake of our children and grandchildren, we empower ourselves. We do something and something changes.

Environmental, economic, political, and social problems are all linked to self-esteem. In understanding the qualities of healthy families—respect, responsibility, caring, awareness of cause-and-effect relationships; setting limits, fixing mistakes and learning from them, and resisting the temptation to "win" if it means damaging others—we understand the principles of healthy societies.

Families are the microcosm of society. If we can create a family in which love and the good of all its members are the common goal, we can create a community in which the same thing happens. If prejudice, violence, and economic injustice stem even partially from low self-esteem, imagine what a world would look like in which people knew their worth. Imagine a future in which leaders are no longer motivated by greed, vengeance, power, and conquest, in which human rights are honored and everyone is free to pursue their own happiness.

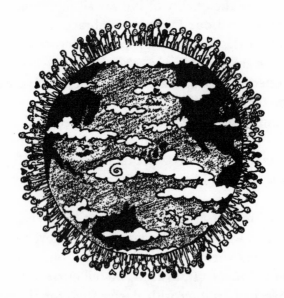

"Only a person or nation self-confident in the best sense of the word is able to listen to the voice of others and to accept them as equal to oneself. Let us try to introduce the self-confidence . . . into the life of our community . . . and into the international scene."[2]

Vaclav Havel

Self-esteem begins in the family, but does not stop there. The principles in this book for building winning families apply to all human situations. Boys and girls who learn to love themselves and others will mature to influence those around them in positive ways. Children with high self-esteem are the greatest gifts parents can give to a world that will one day be theirs. Because, ultimately, there is only one winning family.

Appendix A

100 + Ways to Praise and Encourage a Child

Wow! • Way to Go • Super • You're Special • Outstanding • Great Excellent • Good • Neat • Well Done • Remarkable • I Knew You Could Do It • I'm Proud of You • Fantastic • Super Star • Nice Work • Looking Good • You're On Top of It • Beautiful • Now You're Flying • You're Catching On • Now You've Got It • You're Incredible • Bravo • You're Fantastic • Hurray for You • You're on Target • You're on Your Way • How Nice • You're Smart • Good Job • That's Incredible • Hot Dog • Dynamite • You're Beautiful • You're Unique • Nothing Can Stop You Now • Much Better • Good for You • I Like You • I Like What You Do • I'm Impressed • You Are Clever • You're a Winner • Remarkable Job • Beautiful Work • Spectacular • You're Precious • You're Darling • You're Terrific • Atta Boy • Atta Girl • Congratulations • You've Discovered the Secret • You Figured It Out • Hip, Hip, Hurray! • I Appreciate Your Help • You're Getting Better • Yeah! • Magnificent • Marvelous • Terrific • You Are Important • Phenomenal • You Are Sensational • Super Work • You're Very Creative • You're a Real Trooper • You Are Fun • Did Good • What an Imagination • I Like the Way You Listen • I Like How You're Growing • I Enjoy You • You Tried Hard • You Care • You Are So Thoughtful • Beautiful Sharing • Outstanding Performance • You Are a Good Friend • I Trust You • You Are Important • You Mean a Lot to Me • That's Correct • You're a Joy You're a Treasure • You're Wonderful • Awesome • A+ Job • You Did Your Best • You're A-OK • My Buddy • You Made My Day I'm Glad You Are My Kid • Thanks for Being You • I Love You!

Also: A Pat on the Back • A Big Hug • A Kiss •
A Thumbs-Up Sign • A Warm Smile

Adapted from material from Charter Hospital, Tucson, Arizona.

Appendix B

New Rules for Kids

It's okay
to trust your eyes and ears
to think what you think
to feel and express feelings
to want what you want
to play and have fun

It's crucial
to delay gratification, to know limits
to have a conscience
to tell the truth
to be responsible and learn from the consequences
to know that problems are natural, and mistakes are teachers

Adapted from "Bradshaw: On Homecoming,"
a television series by John Bradshaw.

Appendix C

Leadership Styles

	Autocratic Style	Democratic Style	Permissive Style
Characteristics of Parents	• Keep (overuse) power • Impose will through rigid rules • Little flexibility, freedom • Use force, pressure and punishment • Demand "respect" (fear) • Make all decisions/ rules; demand compliance • Only one right way • Feelings ignored	• Share power • Lead with kindness and firmness • Treat others with respect; flexibility • Treat kids as responsible, worthwhile human beings • Encourage kids to make decisions, think for themselves • Let kids be who they are, do things their way	• Abdicate power • No rules, structure; chaos results • Too much freedom • Believe they have no rights • Absent (physically or emotionally), or are simply not interested
Feelings of Parents	• Superior (one-up) and "in control" • Untrusting of children • Afraid of environment • Lonely; low self-esteem • Burdened with responsibility	• In charge, yet flexible • Respectful, cooperative • Trusting of self & kids • Sensitive to others' feelings • High self-esteem	• Powerless, out of control • Confused and angry • Disrespected • Low self-esteem

Autocratic Style	Democratic Style	Permissive Style
• Powerless, out of control • Untrusting, guilty • Hostile and angry • Dependent and submissive • Afraid, unsafe • Low self-esteem	• Worthwhile, important • Self-confident, self-respecting • Trusted and respected • Eager to cooperate • Safe • High self-esteem	• Unloved • Confused, discouraged • Dependent, rejected • Can't cope with routine • Low self-esteem • Powerless, out of control
• Lack a sense of personal responsibility • Self-rejecting and lonely • Compliant or defiant • Second-guessing common • Always feel one-down, even when grown	• Responsible, respectful • Self-disciplined • Self-determining • Understand cause-effect relationships • Can be friends, equals with parents	• Don't respect feelings of others • Think they have a right to do exactly as they wish • Little awareness of social reponsibility • Have trouble with limits, yet hunger for them

Appendix D

The Power of Expectations

Daddy expects me to be grown up.
If I prove to him that I am grown up,
he will love me.
But I feel frightened
because I am just a little kid.
And I feel terrified that he will
find out that I am frightened
and not grown up
and will not love me.
So I pretend not to be terrified
and he is proud of my being
what I am not.
Now he thinks that I am grown up
and I breathe a sigh of relief.
But now that I am who I am not,
he expects me to be even more of who
I am not, which terrifies me all the more
because I am now expected to be more of
someone I never was.
To complicate matters, he says I should never lie.
So if I tell him that I am not grown up,
he will be proud of my telling him the truth.
But I cannot tell the truth
about not telling the truth
because that is admitting to a lie.
Therefore, I must try harder
to be who I am not.

Anonymous

Appendix E

Locus of Control

External	**Internal**
Listen mostly to outside voices ("should," "have to").	Listen mostly to inner voices, intuition ("want to," "choose to").
Live life based on who they are supposed to be.	Live life based on who they are.
Avoid personal responsibility; then when something goes wrong, can blame others.	Accept responsibility for themselves, for their behaviors, and the consequences.
Trust others more. Look to others to take charge, to take care of them.	Trust themselves, yet listen to others. Take charge of their own lives.
Have more confidence in others than in themselves.	Have increasing self-confidence.
Are vulnerable to pressure, manipulation, exploitation.	Think and make their own decisions; can resist external forces.
Give power away, then feel powerless.	Have a sense of personal power.
Feel helpless, out of control, like victims.	Feel in control of life; are pulling their own strings.
Worry about what their peers or neighbors think.	Care more about what they themselves think.
Have low self-esteem.	Have high self-esteem.

Appendix F

Choose the way of life.
Choose the way of love.
Choose the way of caring.
Choose the way of hope.
Choose the way of belief in tomorrow.
Choose the way of trusting.
Choose the way of goodness.
It's up to you. It's your choice.[1]

Leo F. Buscaglia

Resources Available to Parents

Often during the years of parenting, I felt very isolated. I did not know how to make friends, or how to be a friend. (Talking only about husbands and kids as I'd learned to do is not a basis for friendship.) At that time, I also did not appreciate the importance of friendships, especially when relatives are distant. I was not aware that it was my responsibility to reach out, to find, to create supports. I now know that I am responsible for developing the self-support, people-support, and system-support that I need.

Though I felt isolated, I was, in fact, not alone. There were thousands of people around me, but I didn't have the self-confidence, assertiveness, or people-skills to ask for what I needed. My hope, in writing this book, is to teach you those skills and to encourage you to reach out to others—for friendship, for fun, for support. Don't be afraid to ask for help or support! *You are not alone.*

- Create your own group. With a few friends, you can fashion exactly what you want for yourself.
- Many churches and temples are family oriented. If yours is not, express your needs. Ask for the support you want. Your needs are not yours alone but are shared by others.

- Classes, workshops, counseling, and support are available for parents through community agencies, community colleges, and parenting centers.

If you have difficulty locating what you need, your county mental health center should have information on local resources. Remember, whatever you're looking for, you'll find.

If you feel overwhelmed at times, don't panic. Sometimes what you need is to get away from the kids for a while—walk in the woods, visit a friend, go dancing—to help you relax and regain perspective.

Take good care of yourself because I'm counting on you to take good care of your children.

Recommended Reading

Black, Claudia. *It Will Never Happen to Me.* Denver: M.A.C. Publishers, 1982. Information on alcoholic family systems.

Briggs, Dorothy Corkille. *Your Child's Self-Esteem.* New York: Doubleday, 1970. The first book on self-esteem in children.

Clarke, Jean Illsley. *Self-Esteem: A Family Affair.* Minneapolis, Minn.: Winston Press, 1978. Lists affirmations to use on your kids—and yourself.

Dinkmeyer, Donald, and Gary D. McKay. *The Parent's Handbook: Systematic Training for Effective Parenting.* Circle Pines, Minn.: American Guidance Service, 1982. If after reading *The Winning Family* you still have trouble with discipline, read this book or take a S.T.E.P. class.

Faber, Adele, and Elaine Mazlish. *How to Talk So Kids Will Listen and Listen So Kids Will Talk.* New York: Avon Books, 1980. A best-selling book on family communication.

Faber, Adele, and Elaine Mazlish. *Siblings Without Rivalry.* New York: Avon Books, 1987. For further help in teaching children how to get along.

Fanning, Tony, and Robbie Fanning. *Get It All Done and Still Be Human.* Menlo Park, Calif.: Kali House, 1990. A helpful guide to understanding and organizing the many roles of a parent.

Gil, Eliana. *Outgrowing the Pain*. New York: Dell Publishers, 1983 Can help to heal an abusive childhood.

Green, Christopher. *Toddler Taming*. New York: Ballantine Books, 1984. Wisdom and humor to help get through toddlerhood.

Lerner, Harriet Goldhor. *The Dance of Anger*. New York: Harper and Row, 1985. Recommended if you have trouble dealing with anger.

Palmer, Patricia. *Liking Myself* (for ages 5–9), *The Mouse, the Monster, and Me* (for ages 8–12), *Teen Esteem* (for teenagers). San Luis Obispo, Calif.: Impact Publishers, 1977, 1977, 1989. Wonderful books for youngsters of all ages.

Turecki, Stanley, and Leslie Tonner. *The Difficult Child*. New York: Bantam Books, 1989. For understanding and managing hard-to-raise children.

Notes

CHAPTER 2

1. Henry David Thoreau, quoted in *2,715 One-Liner Quotations for Speakers, Writers and Raconteurs* by Edward F. Murphy (New York: Crown Publishers, 1981).

2. From a lecture by Foster Cline, adult and child psychiatrist, Evergreen, Colo., 1976.

3. This and other comments on children with special needs added with thanks to speech language pathologist Dawn Graves Guderian, M.S., C.C.C.

CHAPTER 3

1. Eleanor Roosevelt, *This Is My Story* (New York: Harper and Brothers, 1937.)

2. Affirmation from Jack Canfield tapes, *Self-Esteem: The Key to Success,* a six-cassette album available from Self-Esteem Seminars, 17156 Palisades Circle, Pacific Palisades, Calif. 90272.

3. Quoted in *2,715 One-Liner Quotations for Speakers, Writers and Raconteurs* by Edward F. Murphy (New York: Crown Publishers, 1981).

CHAPTER 4

1. Eric Hoffer, quoted in *Bits and Pieces* (Fairfield, N.J.: Economics Press, 1986).

2. Samual Osherson, "Finding Our Fathers," *Utne Reader* (April/May 1986).

3. Mildred Newman and Bernard Berkowitz with Jean Owen, *How to Be Your Own Best Friend* (New York: Random House, 1973).

4. Leo F. Buscaglia, Ph.D., *Living, Loving and Learning* (Thorofare, N.J.: Slack, Inc., 1982). Used by permission.

CHAPTER 5

1. John Powell, *The Secret of Staying in Love* (Allen, Tex.: Argus Communications, 1974).

2. Julie Rigg and Julie Copeland, *Coming Out! Women's Voices, Women's Lives* (Melbourne N.S.W., Australia: Nelson Press, 1985).

3. Parent Effectiveness Training (P.E.T.) teaches listening skills based on Rogerian counseling principles.

4. Leo F. Buscaglia, Ph.D., *Loving Each Other* (Thorofare, N.J.: Slack Inc., 1984). Used by permission.

CHAPTER 6

1. Virginia Mae Axline, *Dibs: In Search of Self* (Boston: Houghton Mifflin, 1964).

2. Concepts adapted from Dr. Pat Palmer, *The Mouse, the Monster and Me* (San Luis Obispo, Calif.: Impact Publishers, 1977).

3. Ibid.

4. "Saying 'no' means . . ." and "the value of no . . ." exercise from Claudia Black, *It Will Never Happen to Me* (Denver, Colo.: M.A.C. Publications, 1982).

CHAPTER 7

1. Anne Morrow Lindbergh, quoted in Murphy, *2,715 One-Liner Quotations,* loc. cit.

2. Dorothy Corkille Briggs, *Building Self-Esteem in Children* (Garden City, N.Y.: Doubleday, 1975).

3. Black, *It Will Never Happen to Me*, loc. cit.

4. Personal friend, Laurel Hameon, Australia, 1992.

5. Henry David Thoreau, quoted in Murphy, *2,715 One-Liner Quotations,* loc. cit.

6. Minnesota Student Services Report, 1989 (900,000 students).

7. T. Gordon, *Parent Effectiveness Training* (New York: Wyden, 1973).

8. Concepts expanded from Briggs, *Building Self-Esteem in Children,* loc. cit.

9. *American Heritage Dictionary* (New York: Dell 1976).

10. Guderian, loc. cit., and Diane Frey and C. Jesse Carlock, Ph.D., *Enhancing Self-Esteem*, 2nd ed. (Muncie, Ind.: Accelerated Development Inc., 1989).

11. Philip Oliver-Diaz and Patricia O'Gorman, *12 Steps to Self-Parenting* (Deerfield Beach, Fla.: Health Communications, 1988).

12. John James and Frank Cherry, *The Grief Recovery Handbook* (New York: HarperCollins, 1989).

13. Buscaglia, *Loving Each Other*, loc. cit.

14. Concept from Canfield *Self-Esteem* tapes, loc. cit.

15. Lewis B. Smedes, *Forgive and Forget* (New York: Pocket Books/ Simon and Schuster, 1984).

16. Clyde Reid, *Celebrate the Temporary* (New York: Harper and Row, 1972).

17. Matthew Fox, *Meditations with Meister Eckhart* (Santa Fe, N.M.: Bear and Co., 1983).

18. Chart excerpted from Gilda Gussin and Anne Buxbaum, *Self-Discovery: Developing Skills* (Boston: Learning for Life, Management Sciences for Health, 1984).

CHAPTER 8

1. Matthew Fox, *Original Blessing* (Santa Fe, N.M.: Bear and Co., 1983).

2. Concepts adapted from Jean Illsley Clarke, *Self-Esteem: A Family Affair* (Minneapolis: Winston Press, 1978).

3. Ibid.

4. Gordon, *Parent Effectiveness Training*, loc. cit., p. 45.

CHAPTER 9

1. Robert Ricker, *Love Me When I'm Most Unlovable* (Reston, Va.: National Association of Secondary School Principals).

2. Concepts adapted from Jean Illsley Clarke, *Self-Esteem*, loc. cit.

CHAPTER 10

1. Albert Schweitzer, quoted in Murphy, *2,715 One-Liner Quotations*, loc. cit.

CHAPTER 11

1. Marilyn French, *Beyond Power—On Women, Men, and Morals* (New York: Ballantine Books, 1985).

2. Personal friend, name withheld, 1982.

CHAPTER 12

1. Kaleel Jamison, *The Nibble Theory and the Kernel of Power* (New York: Paulist Press, 1984).

2. Mary Fran Gilleran, I.H.M., "Blowing the Whistle on Oppression," *Kindred Spirits Newsletter*, Detroit, Mich., Vol. 6, No. 3, Jan./Feb. 1988.

3. Kathleen Hallahan, "Why So Violent?", *Foundation News*, May/June 1986.

4. "Child Injury Deaths," *American Journal for Public Health*, Vol. 79, March 1989.

5. Anthony V. Bouza, "The Epidemic of Family Violence," *Surgeon General's Workshop on Violence and Public Health Report* (Washington, D.C.: Health Resources and Services Administration, U.S. Public Health Service, 1986).

6. Paula Gunn Allen, "Connecting with the Source," *Creation*, Vol. 2, No. 6, Jan./Feb. 1987.

7. For more information on Parent Action, write to 2 Hopkins Plaza, Baltimore, Md. 21201, or call (410) 752-1790.

8. Dr. T. Berry Brazelton, quoted in *Chicago Tribune Tempo*, Oct. 21, 1988.

CHAPTER 13

1. *Pot Shots* cartoon #2369 by Ashleigh Brilliant (Santa Barbara, Calif.: Brilliant Enterprises, 1982)

2. Concepts adapted from Donald Dinkmeyer and Gary D. McKay, *The Parents Handbook: Systematic Training for Effective Parenting* (Circle Pines, Minn.: American Guidance Service, 1982).

3. H. S. Glenn and B. J. Wagner, *Developing Capable People*, instructor's manual. Privately printed. Undated.

4. Kenneth Blanchard and Spencer Johnson, *The One-Minute Manager* (New York: Berkley Books, 1981).

5. Lao Tzu, *Tao Te Ching: A New English Version*, translated by Stephen Mitchell (New York: Harper & Row, 1988).

CHAPTER 14

1. Garrison Keillor, on "Prairie Home Companion," broadcast on National Public Radio, July 2, 1989.

2. *1992 Information, Please! Almanac Atlas/Yearbook*, 45th ed., (Boston: Houghton Mifflin, 1992).

3. From an article in *Young Children Magazine*, July 1990, National Association for the Education of Young Children.

4. *1992 Information, Please!*, loc. cit.

5. *USA Today*, January 21, 1985.

6. *USA Today*, September 11, 1986.

7. From an article in *Young Children Magazine*, July 1990, National Association for the Education of Young Children.

CHAPTER 15

1. Jo Coudert, *Advice from a Failure* (Briarcliff Manor, N.Y.: Stein and Day Publishers, 1965).

2. Personal friend, name withheld, 1982.

3. Jesse Jackson, from a speech to the Denver Public Schools Push/Excel Program, August 1979.

4. Richard Bach, *Illusions* (New York: Delacorte Press, 1977).

CHAPTER 16

1. Statement made by author's son Felix at age 13.

2. Attributed to the late Virginia Satir.

3. J. W. Prescott, "Body Pleasure and the Origins of Violence," *The Futurist*, April 1975.

4. Jules Older, Ph.D. "A Restoring Touch for Abusing Families." *The International Journal of Child Abuse and Neglect*, Vol. 5, No. 4 (1981). Exercise devised by occupational therapist Franceska Banga.

5. Exercise adapted by Martha Belknap.

6. For information on P.R.E.S., contact Jeanne St. John, Ph.D., Director, Santa Cruz County Office of Education, 809 Bay Avenue, Suite H, Capitola, Calif. 95010.

7. Attributed to George Santayana, and quoted in William Shirer's *The Rise and Fall of the Third Reich* (New York: Simon and Schuster, 1960).

8. Linda Tschirhart Sanford, *The Silent Children* (Garden City, N.Y.: Anchor Press/Doubleday, 1980).

9. Brandt F. Steele, quoted in *St. Louis Post-Dispatch*, August 8, 1982.

10. Personal friend, name withheld, 1986.

11. *A Course in Miracles* (Tiburon, Calif.: Foundation for Inner Peace, 1975).

CHAPTER 17

1   Henry Ford, quoted by Louis Tice in audiotape "New Age Thinking for Achieving Your Potential" (Seattle, Wash.: Pacific Institute).

CHAPTER 18

1. Quoted in *Sunbeams, A Book of Quotations,* by Sy Safransky (Berkeley, Calif.: Sun Publishing Co., 1990).

2. Some concepts adapted from Matthew McKay, Martha Davis, and Patrick Fanning, *The Art of Cognitive Stress Intervention* (Richmond, Calif.: New Harbinger Publications, 1981).

CHAPTER 19

1. Quoted in Safransky, *Sunbeams,* loc. cit.

2. Frey and Carlock, Ph.D., *Enhancing Self-Esteem,* loc. cit.

CHAPTER 20

1. Gloria Steinem, "A New Egalitarian Life Style," *The New York Times,* August 26, 1971.

2. Barry and Janae Weinhold, *Breaking Free of the Co-Dependency Trap* (Walpole, N.H.: Stillpoint, 1989).

3. Clarke, *Self-Esteem,* loc. cit.

4. Jane Fonda, *New Workout and Weight-Loss Program* (New York: Simon and Schuster, 1986).

5. Marilyn Ferguson, *The Aquarian Conspiracy: Personal and Social Transformation in the 80s* (Los Angeles: J. P. Tarcher, 1976).

CHAPTER 21

1. e. e. cummings, quoted in *The Magic-Maker,* by Charles Norman (New York: Macmillan, 1958).

2. Attributed to psychologist Albert Ellis.

3. Bernie Siegel, *Love, Medicine, and Miracles* (New York: Harper and Row, 1986).

4. Ferguson, *The Aquarian Conspiracy,* loc. cit.

5. Joseph Campbell, *The Power of Myth* (New York: Doubleday, 1988).

CHAPTER 22

1. Quoted in Safransky, *Sunbeams,* loc. cit.

2. See Andrew Fluegelman, *The New Games Book* (New York: Doubleday, 1974).

3. Norman Cousins, *Anatomy of an Illness* (New York: Norton, 1979).

CHAPTER 23

1. Barbara Sher, *Wishcraft: How to Get What You Really Want* (New York: Viking Press, 1979).

2. Ibid.

CHAPTER 24

1. Bach, *Illusions,* loc. cit.

2. U.S. Current Population Reports, *Geographical Mobility,* March 83–March 84, Series P20 #407 (Washington, D.C.: U.S. Department of Commerce, Bureau of the Census).

3. *The Greeley* [Colorado] *Tribune,* January 11, 1978, and information from an interview with Bessie Cohea, 1982.

CHAPTER 25

1. Quotation on a patchwork quilt expanded by Denis Waitly.

2. Roly-poly, also known as the sow bug or pill bug: any of various small, terrestrial crustaceans of the genus Armadillidum or related genera, having convex, segmented bodies capable of being curled into a ball.

Top view   Side view   Rolling

CHAPTER 26

1. Quoted in Safransky, *Sunbeams,* loc. cit.

2. President Vaclav Havel, in his acceptance speech to the people of Czechoslovakia, New Year's Day, 1990.

APPENDIX F

1. Buscaglia, *Living, Loving and Learning,* loc. cit.

Index

Index

nurturing response, 82–84, 84–85
structuring response, 82–84, 85
Perfectionism, 14, 46, 51, 57, 179–86
alternatives to, 183–86
difficulties related to, 180–82
and dissatisfaction, 68
Permissive leadership style, 95, 98–100
children's characteristics, 99
children's feelings, 99–100
parental characteristics, 100
parental feelings, 101
Physical punishment, 127, 155, 159
Play, 218–24
for adults, 218–19
and discipline, 126
and immune system, 222–23
and learning, 220
parent/child play, 221–22
and TV, 138
Power
associations, 106–7
and child abuse, 159
dimensions of, 109
games, 107–8
sharing with children, 103
Proactive leadership, 89–90, 91–92
Problem solving, 141–50
barriers to, 145–46
guidelines for, 147–49
listening and, 148
and self-esteem, 142
steps to, 149–50
win-lose approach, 146
win-win approach, 107, 146–49
Protection skills, for negative
influences, 21–24
Put-down, self, 170, 190–91

R

Rage, 63
Reactive leadership, 90–91, 91–92
Refusing skills, communicating, 42–44
Relationships
always pleasing others, 9, 123,
193–94
objectification, 205–10
over-responsibility for others,
142–43, 195–96

Reparenting yourself, 3, 12–13, 47–48,
110, 227
Rescue behavior, 119–20
Resentment, 64
Reward/punishment system, 121–23
disadvantages of, 122–23, 126–27
options to, 123–26

S

Safety, sense of, 25, 46, 143
Self-awareness
and beliefs, 163
and changing behavior, 3–4, 172
and child abuse, 156, 160
and criticism, 72, 176
and parental self-discipline, 127
and turnabout statements, 80
and writing, 64
Self-care, exercise for, 31, 32, 192–93
Self-defeating behavior
alcoholic family systems, 199–200
avoidance, 145, 197–98
body image and, 196–97
comparison, 202–5
dualistic thinking, 78, 200–2
faulty thinking, 173–76
objectification, 205–210
over-responsibility for others,
142–43, 195–96
pleasing others (always), 9, 123,
193–94
self-sacrifice, 189, 192–93
self put-downs, 170, 190–91
separating person from behavior,
78, 200–2
sexism/racism, 205–7
win-lose system, 108, 146, 202–4,
210–11
Self-discipline, parental, 127
Self-esteem
development in children, 10–13
from external sources, 8, 9
high self-esteem, sources of, 9, 15
increasing, exercise for, 17–18
low self-esteem, sources of, 14
and making mistakes, 120, 123–24,
180, 183–86

VIDEOTAPE

Win-Win Kids in a Win-Lose World is an opportunity to "attend" Dr. Hart's popular workshop on building self-esteem in children. She speaks to an audience of parents, educators, and child-care providers.

AUDIOTAPES

Building Self-Esteem in Children
Recorded at Dr. Hart's popular workshop for parents. Topics include: why self-esteem is important; ways to build it; self-esteem protection skills; communicating love; and the power of words.

Increasing Your Own Self-Esteem
How adults can improve their own self-esteem. Discusses the sources of self-esteem; self-talk; self-esteem-building exercises; cultural barriers to self-esteem; locus of control; and saying "no."

BOOKLET

"Self-Esteem: The Best Gift for Your Children . . . and Yourself!"
"Auto-Estima: El Regalo Mejor para sus Hijos . . . ¡y Ustéd!"
An excerpt from this book, written in simple language—available in both English and Spanish. Ideal for child abuse prevention programs, social service agencies, health professionals, teachers, school counselors, and principals. A perfect way to reach out and support parents.

DISCUSSION GUIDE

Written by Dr. Hart with Nevin Saunders of the California Parenting Institute and the director of parenting programs at Napa Community College, this chapter-by-chapter guide contains discussion questions and exercises for parenting groups and teachers using *The Winning Family* as a text.

Order Form

Quantity   **Price**

_____ **Videotape**   **$29.95**
Win-Win Kids in a Win-Lose World

Audiotapes   **$10.00 ea.**
_____ *Building Self-Esteem in Children*
_____ *Increasing Your Own Self-Esteem*

Booklets
_____ "Self-Esteem: The Best Gift for Your
Children . . . and Yourself!"

_____ "Auto-Estima: El Regalo Mejor para
sus Hijos . . . ¡y Ustéd!"

1–9	$2.50 ea.
10–99	$2.00 ea.
100–499	$1.50 ea.
500 or more	$1.00 ea.

_____ **Discussion Guide**   **$7.00**
For parent or teacher discussion groups
using *The Winning Family* as a text

Send check or money order.
California and Colorado residents please add sales tax.
Shipping/handling: Add $2.50 for the first item, 75¢ for each
additional item, or for single booklets.

Name: _____

Ship to: _____

_____

_____

Mail to: LifeSkills Press, P.O. Box 324, Boulder, CO 80306